Kid on the River

By the same author:

- *Islands Of Experience*
- *A Poet's Sketch, Of His Biography*
- *A Sailor's Yarns And Observations*
- *Two Cats For Puerto Rico*
- *The N.P.M.W.A R A.*
- *The Copper Sands*
- *The Highline Trail*

Kid on the
RIVER

REVISED EDITION

by DEAN NICHOLS

RESOURCE *Publications* • Eugene, Oregon

KID ON THE RIVER
Revised Edition

Copyright © 1988, 2013 Dean Nichols. All rights reserved. Except for brief quotations in critical publications or reviews, no part of this book may be reproduced in any manner without prior written permission from the publisher. Write: Permissions. Wipf and Stock Publishers, 199 W. 8th Ave., Suite 3, Eugene, OR 97401.

Resource Publications
An Imprint of Wipf and Stock Publishers
199 W. 8th Ave., Suite 3
Eugene, OR 97401

www.wipfandstock.com

ISBN 13: 978-1-62564-524-1

Manufactured in the U.S.A.

To Captain Luke Nichols

Captain Luke Nichols, 1937

Acknowledgments

My loving gratitude goes to my wife, Ramona, who urged and urged me, "Dean, go to the Oregon Coast that you love, walk those healing sands, and write your story. Only you can do that."

My appreciation goes to Captain Slim Leppaluoto, Captain George Shaver, and Captain Lew Russel. They gave me encouragement—and a few corrections.

Contents

Introduction / xi

CHAPTER 1 The Race / 1
CHAPTER 2 A Special Loan Program / 6
CHAPTER 3 A Lesson in Prudence / 8
CHAPTER 4 His Heritage / 10
CHAPTER 5 The Willows / 13
CHAPTER 6 Knute / 17
CHAPTER 7 Slim / 23
CHAPTER 8 Bridge of the Gods / 27
CHAPTER 9 The Corbett Light / 29
CHAPTER 10 Lost Love and Lesson Learned / 33
CHAPTER 11 Breakdown at Hamilton Island / 36
CHAPTER 12 Victory at Hamilton Island / 39
CHAPTER 13 Audacity- or Daring? / 42
CHAPTER 14 Bonneville Again / 46
CHAPTER 15 The Dubois Mill / 49
CHAPTER 16 More Funny Things / 51
CHAPTER 17 Sometimes the Bad Guys Won / 56
CHAPTER 18 A Burned Hand / 60
CHAPTER 19 Fog Stories / 63
CHAPTER 20 Other Funny Things / 66
CHAPTER 21 A Magnificent Vessel / 69
CHAPTER 22 Flying Stories / 71
CHAPTER 23 Inventions / 77
CHAPTER 24 The Big Invention / 81
CHAPTER 25 Russell Towboat and Moorage Company / 84
CHAPTER 26 Portland Tug and Barge / 91
CHAPTER 27 The Army / 99
CHAPTER 28 General Construction / 109
CHAPTER 29 The Final Story / 122

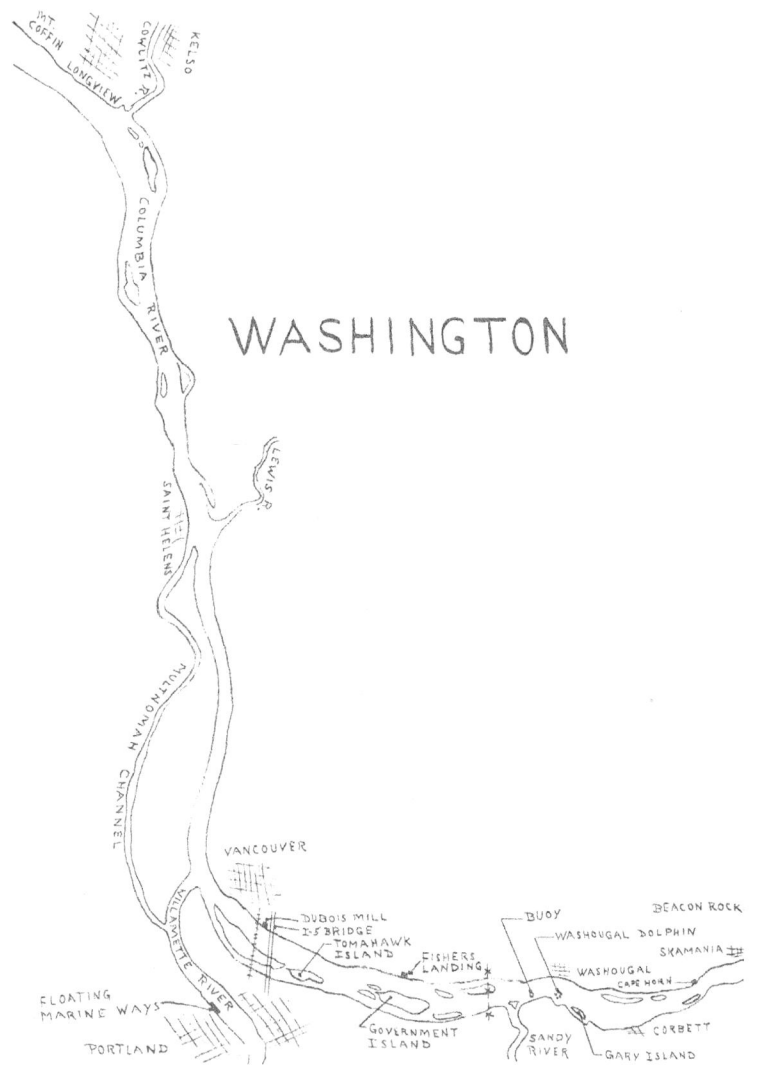

Introduction

I realize, with a sad, yet lovely nostalgia, that the "kid" is gone now; no one will ever see him again, at least not on this earth. Yet he is not gone; he lives, here, in this little book. And because this book will live forever, he will forever live that delightful, daring, innocent, exciting, wise, and sometimes stumbling, but always refreshing life of a kid who owned for a little while, and will belong to forever, the middle stretch of the mighty Columbia River.

Everything mentioned here actually happened. Some may question the precision of its historical accuracy; and that's OK. But to the best of my memory, this is a true story.

And it is deeply hoped that no persons named herein will take offense at what is said or implied about them; or that no relatives of those named, whether living or dead, will take offense.

Most assuredly, no offense is intended.

> *They that go down to*
> *the sea in ships, who*
> *do business in great*
> *waters, these see*
> *the works of the Lord*
> *and His wonders in the deep.*
> Ps. 107:23–24.

Chapter 1
The Race

July 1979: The screaming engines had quieted some, as the big plane made its last turn before settling on final approach to Portland International Airport. We were crossing the Columbia, and as always, I scanned the water for some memory, some small link with the past. There, that small tug, with a single log raft, plodding down that great waterway. I smiled and remembered a kid I once knew, a boy tugboat captain, and then I openly grinned as the story of a tugboat race he had had, over 40 years before, came rushing back into my mind.

The mid-Columbia, or, as some prefer, Bonneville Lake, some 60 to 80 miles east of Portland, is almost always rough. The summer heating of the inland semi-desert builds a standing low-pressure system that, with the cooler, Pacific air west of the Cascade Mountains, sets up a pressure gradient not unlike the difference in pressure inside and outside a balloon, the Columbia Gorge being the opened neck of that balloon. The old, flat log rafts did not survive well in those six- to eight-foot, and higher, waves. So most log towing was done at night.

The Underwood Log Dump, across the Columbia from Hood River, Oregon, July 1939, 2:00 A.M. It was a clear, but very dark night, as the kid stepped aboard his 38-foot, 60 hp tug and started the engine, a "high-speed" Atlas diesel. High speed, because it turned 600 rpms instead of the usual 300 to 350 rpms of the old, heavy-duty engines.

He had a single log raft to tow to Vancouver, Washington. The raft was already rigged with extra lines called swifters and doglines, so it was only moments before the raft was free, the towline hooked, and that tiny engine was barking at full throttle as the raft followed out into the dark night.

Les Egan, the part-time deckhand, part-time recluse, often crotchety, but as often entertaining friend, brought coffee to the wheelhouse. "The towline is tied down, Skipper, looks like we have an easy night."

"Yes," replied the kid, "It's tough to be up at these ungodly hours, in a way, but there is peace and beauty too. You know, Les, I believe I've seen more sunrises, really glorious sunrises, than most people have sunsets. Seems like everything has its compensations."

Les agreed, and returned some philosophical observation. But a half hour later he noted, "Looks like we have company; looks like one of the Smith tugs a couple miles back with a raft out of Hood River."

A few hours later, as the colors of dawn were beginning to grace the eastern sky, the Smith tug was nearly abreast of the kid. With his 120 hp Cummins diesel, he had twice the horsepower. It was making a difference. By the time they had passed Wind River, he was clearly ahead.

"You know, Les, if they make the locks (Bonneville Locks) before we do we'll just have to wait an hour and a half or so while they lock through. But, I don't know what we can do; he just has us out powered."

But an hour later, the kid noted something. The Smith tug was taking the usual route, a sort of shortcut behind an island a mile or so east of the old Cascade Locks.

"You know, Les," the kid reasoned, "I've always taken that route too, because it is obviously shorter. But if we follow him, we know we are beat. I'm going to stay out

in the main river, even if it is longer. Maybe the extra current will give us a break."

The Race

Another hour passed by, and as the two tugs cleared the island, and came in sight of each other again, the kid was a half mile ahead.

With the building of Bonneville Dam, the old Cascade Rapids were covered with quieter water. Still, the current picked up two or three miles per hour in speed from there to Bonneville. Whoever reached the rapids first, would, of course, reach the locks first. The race would be over. But there was still one more mile to go.

"Hey, he's worried," shouted Les. "Look at that black smoke." That Cummins was obviously screaming.

"Les, get down in the engine room and put your foot on the wedges," shouted the kid, "We can't lose this race now."

On those old Atlas diesels, the engine speed was controlled by a governor, which controlled a row of wedges that pushed in or out to increase or decrease the lift on the external pushrods, increasing or decreasing the opening of the nozzles spraying fuel into the cylinders. It was an easy thing to sit on the edge of the combing in the engine room and put one's foot on one of the wedges, forcing them all in their full depth.

Les dove for the engine room; and that little engine was now turning 900 rpms, nearly doubling her power. Black smoke was filling the sky from two stacks now.

An eternity passed, as the two tiny engines roared, two young captains leaned slightly forward, urging their steeds along.

But the Smith tug had made a mistake in the race. And a half-hour later the kid broke into the fast water, and swept away from the contest. The engines settled to their normal rhythms, the black smoke subsided; the race was over.

A tugboat race of long ago, a race lasting half a night, and part of an early dawn. Yet it had flashed through my mind during that final approach to Portland International Airport. And as the tires screeched in contact with the runway, I came back to the present, to now. But that grin stayed with me; and though no one asked about it, a few noted that gray-haired man, obviously in his own world, and smiling broadly at his memories.

A Sailor's Two Loves

There is a sweet and gently painful loneliness on the sea, somewhat akin to nostalgia, and although on this trip aboard the *M/V Brant* it was generally well suppressed by the company of two biologists, both lively and friendly extroverts, these men would sometimes leave the ship for half a day at a time, and the full awareness of the sailor's loneliness would have the free course to come to the surface and be known.

And thus it was one long Alaskan afternoon, in the heart of this mountain-torn sea, as I sat down in the silence, alone, to write a letter in:

Anderson Bay
Hinchinbrook Island
Prince William Sound
Alaska
August 29, 1965

My beloved family,
    The thunder of silence is almost deafening, and would be so were it not for the occasional dampening effect of the sound of a raven's call, or the cry of a gull, or the patter of rain drops on the deck, or the rush of an almost imperceptible ground swell on a low gravel bar.
    Why is it we find it so necessary, so often, to disturb that perfect harmony of all sound, the silence, with artificial sounds of our own, which at best are but distortions of the silence?
    Only when we stand in the silence, alone, can we be really aware of standing at the meeting place of two eternities, the past and the future, and look at the mountains as they were in the long past and will be in the distant future, but mostly as they are, here, now, in the only reality, the thundering, powerfully eternal and silent present.
    And suddenly I am aware that I miss my family; that the magnetic bond that ties a family together has been pulling its slight but persistent, elastic yet indestructible strand, and the burden, like a pail of water carried in the

hand, becomes increasingly heavy to bear the longer it is borne.

Yet through the mist that shrouds but never completely hides the future, I see myself in the warmth and glow and joy of my family, and I hear another sound, the voice of a siren, the call of the sea; and I know I will have to leave that love for another even before I have returned to my own.

And so it is with those who love the sea; cursed, or blessed (Who is to say?) with two loves, where the wonder of each is somehow magnified by possession of the other; and the sailor finds himself with one plea: love him and let him love you. His love is sweeter, greater, more to be cherished for his other love, and he needs the silence and distance of the sea wherein that love can grow and expand and show itself to him in purity and in power.

Love,
Dad Nichols
Captain, *M/V Brant*

From the book, *Islands of Experience,*
by the same author

Chapter 2

A Special Loan Program

Perhaps 10 years after "The Race," the kid and a young partner were aboard a small, gas tug, with a small log raft for Bonneville. It had been a lovely day, warm, with a light east breeze all the way from Hood River.

But a few miles above the old Cascade Rapids, that easterly breeze had freshened. It was now a strong wind, rolling the water into potentially destructive waves. The two boys could see the beating the raft was taking; occasionally, swifter lines broke, the raft was losing its ordered shape. The partner was nervous, and spoke his worried concern. But the kid was calm, and relaxed, steering for the beginning of the fast water where the turn could be made, and the storm's fury would be blocked.

By nature, the kid was not that emotionally unaffected a young man. It was just that he had learned, through hard years, that when all avenues but one were blocked, to hold onto faith, to put his trust in a power beyond ourselves, to conserve his emotional energies, relax, and grin. On a different plane, his mind had already considered the possibility of the destruction of his small tow, and had set that possibility on the shelf as just that, a possibility, but not worthy of worry—yet.

Tugboating is generally a fairly routine science, with clear margins for safe operation. Occasionally, however, the elements do not cooperate with the captain's judgment, and he gets caught

A Special Loan Program

with no margins left. But the kid had learned that if he had been faithful to the rules of good judgment in his daily work, that God allowed him to borrow into a certain "fudge factor" until he was safe again. The kid never failed to remember that he had accepted a loan, and so paid it back, over a period of time, by more than careful attention to those "rules" until the Spirit within him marked the bill paid in full.

By all the laws of chance, over his many years on the water, the kid should have been killed, many times. But he clearly had a good "loan program" going with what some would call "fate." He never over-extended his credit, and he paid off his loans with great care.

At one time, the kid could have named off twenty-five or more men whom he had known personally, and who had lost their lives to the great river. One was a deckhand he was unable to reach, and who went down right before his eyes at, ironically, Mt. Coffin, on the lower Columbia. Another was his skipper who vanished, early on a frosty morning just before a construction crew for the new The Dalles bridge was due to come aboard. The kid had to take over as the new captain. A week later, the kid found the body of his captain a mile or so down river. Bruises indicated he had slipped and fallen between the steel tug and the steel barge while the kid was in the engine room. No one saw him fall.

The kid checked his mooring lines to that higher power very carefully, and for a long time, after each of those experiences.

But what about this day, this storm? Well, less than an hour later the fast water caught them, and swept them around the bend; the river was again a flat, flowing ribbon. When they tied up a mile further down, it took less than an hour to repair the damage, leaving the raft ready for the next tug to tow away.

Chapter 3
A Lesson in Prudence

The Sandy River empties into the Columbia across from Camas and Washougal, Washington. And it has obviously been doing so for a few thousand years. Every flood season it dumps its burden of sand and gravel that it had torn from the mountains of its birth into the heart of the big river, forcing, century by century, the course of the big river farther and farther north.

By the time the kid was there with his tiny tugs, the channel made nearly a mile swing to the north around the Sandy River Bar. A big, black bundle of piling, called the Washougal Dolphin, marked the northeast corner, and a Nun buoy the northwest corner, more or less. There was no problem clearing the dolphin, because the current really swung the log rafts by. And besides, it just might break the rafts to hit that dolphin. But the nun buoy was a little different. If a log raft ran over it, it would just lie down into the water and bump along under the logs.

With the low-powered tugs of those days, they always swung as close to the lower corner of the Sandy River Bar as possible in order to get into position to clear the power line towers in the middle of the river a mile or so farther down. Often it would mean dragging the rafts over that red buoy.

I don't know if the kid knew when the U.S. Coast Guard changed the buoy to a lighted one or not; but he continued to drag

A Lesson in Prudence

his rafts over that buoy. After all, it was less threatening than those massive towers farther down.

But the Coast Guard felt that this was a little rough on, as well as disrespectful of, their buoys, especially that light on top. So one day they slipped out and took numerous photographs of the process. In due time they ordered the kid's dad, owner of the tugboat company, to a Coast Guard hearing.

There was no question, there were, indeed, excellent photos of the Company tugs, and there were pictures of log rafts dragging over the buoy. The "old man's" mind was racing, "How to get out of this one?"

Before the highly respected officers could close the trap, the kid's dad asked to see the photos again. Enjoying the victory he knew was his, he went through them carefully, one by one. Then he relaxed, sat back in his chair, and said, with his uniquely gentle strength, "Gentlemen, you do indeed have some fine pictures of our tugs; and you have some very good pictures of log rafts over-running that buoy. But you have no pictures that show any of my tugs towing the log rafts that are over-running that buoy. Gentlemen, you have no evidence against us."

I think that even the Coast Guard men were relieved when the commanding officer dismissed the case. But the kid felt it prudent to show more respect for U.S. Government property after that.

Chapter 4

His Heritage

The kid's dad was a giant of a man. He was not so tall, but he was powerful, physically, yes, and mentally powerful, with a strength and stamina of some renowned "men of old." But he saw the future, he really saw it, so clearly, sometimes, that the more "practical" ones around were unable to respond but as to a dreamer. In fact, it was in Anchorage, Alaska, about 1979, that the kid, a grown man now, was attending a convention of the Northwest Waterways Association. An old member of the Hood River Port Commission came up and said, "You know, 20 years ago, when your father was living, and a member of the Hood River Port Commission, he was so far ahead of the rest of us that we got lost; we couldn't even dream his dreams. But when you look at the Port of Hood River today, you will see it exactly as your dad dreamed." I'm sure there were tears in the eyes of a great man's son about then.

But in his day-to-day living, that great man's visions did interfere with, or sap away energy that perhaps would have been better spent on the job at hand. Or another way of saying it: the job at hand was so easy for him, he often neglected to follow through. So he never was a really "successful" businessman.

Still, he was a pioneer whose fertile imagination spawned so many new and innovative ideas on the Columbia. His birth and youth were on a Minnesota farm, the breeding ground of many fine mechanics and men of ingenuity.

His Heritage

He spent his years as a mechanic, a trucker, and then, in the early '20s, moved his family to the mid-Columbia area where he developed a reputation as a good logger. But the sawmills in the Bingen–White Salmon area were dominated by one man who did not hesitate to use his monopoly against the loggers, that is, until he tried the same arrogant tactics on this daring, imaginative Minnesota farm boy.

So the kid's dad drove the long, winding, gravel road to Portland, and asked around. Yes, there were mills there who would buy his logs, and, at a much higher price than the Bingen timber baron would pay. But this was years before Bonneville Dam was built. No one had ever successfully towed logs through the Cascade Locks and the several miles of fast water below them.

Ah, but that was the challenge. The river, history, and a lumber baron had thrown down the glove; the giant had a goal that focused that fine mind, and all that energy. He was about to make history. He bought boom chains, and pike poles, and rafting wire, and four-inch hand augers, and he hired workmen to hand-bore the four-inch holes in the ends of the boomsticks, the long, small logs that, linked by the chains, make up the boom that holds the logs together to make up a raft.

They dumped the logs on the beach, and rolled them into the water with peaveys, and the boomcats floated and fit the logs together to make up the first raft. The buyer was waiting in Portland, but with 65 miles and a historically impassable stretch of wild river between.

No real tugboats were available to him, so he hired several small fishboats and started down the river. The year was about 1925.

No, the kid's dad was not, then, a tugboatman. But he had courage, imagination, daring, and determination. Personally directing the operation, they hauled that first raft out into the racing current below the Cascade Rapids. It was a real battle, but once they got the raft into the current, and at, or somewhat faster than the speed of the current, they could control their location in the middle of that flow. They had won; the river was on their side, and swept them into history.

I would give an awful lot for a copy of the magazine, *The Westcoast Lumberman* (or *Timberman*), that wrote up the story for what it really was, a history-making event. The kid was then about five or six years old.

Of course, it just followed that the kid's dad went on to be the principal log-boom owner/operator, and then tugboat-fleet owner/operator, on the mid-Columbia for many years.

Oh, a book of its own could be written about this most unique man. But this book is about his son, a boy both blessed and burdened by his inheritance—the mind of his intellectual mother, with her rich curiosity about life and God, and His plan for our lives; and the dreams and beckoning challenges that called his dad. But he had all of this inheritance without the incredible physical strength and stamina of that great man.

This is the story of just a kid on the river, but woven through will always be the powerful influence of his dad.

Chapter 5
The Willows

The waters of the Columbia started seeping into the kid's and his younger brother's veins almost as soon as they started to school. Their dad had moved the family to a little house on the approach to the Hood River–White Salmon Bridge. To deter anyone else from building a competing bridge near there, the Bridge Co. had bought a strip of land a few hundred feet wide and a mile or so above and below the bridge. The boys' dad, still having a residue of farmer's blood in him, rented the land, fenced it, and pastured six to 10 Shetland ponies, and, of course, a cow or two there.

The land included the old White Salmon Steamboat dock, still in quite good condition, and the office and waiting room building which they used for a barn. In the waiting room were several posters, in excellent condition, showing the pictures of the sternwheelers, Bailey Gatzert, and The Dalles City, ready to take passengers to The Dalles for 50¢. The kid knew then that those posters would be worth money in years to come; but, typical kid, he put off preserving them, and time slipped away. But the call of the river had begun. Many years later, he could recall those posters and feel the regret of having lost them.

The dad never did make any money selling Shetland ponies, but those two boys, and friends from school, had healthy fun playing "marshal" and "outlaws" on those ponies.

Kid on the River

Over the years, a strip of willows, 50 to 100 feet wide, and a mile long, grew along the sandy shore, separating the beach from the landside pasture. The outlaws would ride out, all bareback, of course, and hide in the willows. The marshals would then ride out for the capture. But the rules were that a marshal had to pull an outlaw off his horse to effect the capture. It didn't always work out that way, and there was some wild and exciting riding along the sandy banks of that beckoning stream.

The kid also began learning about the God of his mother there. The west wind nearly always came up in the afternoon, and often at 20 to 30 knots, swaying those willows. Some grew to 24 to 30 feet high. The boys would climb up near the tops, and help them sway in the wind. One day, both were in a large willow, and swaying gleefully before the storm. God didn't really design willows for that much work, and this day, this one broke. But on the long fall to the ground, the kid remembered to pray. After the crash, they dusted off the silty sand, checked themselves over, and found not a mark, not a bruise, not a sore spot on their bodies anywhere. The kid learned a great deal of respect for his Guardian Angel that day, an Angel that would save him many, many times in the years ahead.

But climbing in, and riding among them weren't the only things the willows were good for. During the floods in June and July, the river flooded to 50 to 200 feet inside the willows, forming a fairly protected lagoon. The old dock was also slowly breaking up, during those floods, so there was a supply of 4x12 planks along the inner beach. Those were excellent for building rafts.

"Don't you boys play in the river," Mama would call as they ran out to play. So on the way to the river, they would rationalize, as kids still do, "What Mama really means is, 'Don't do anything really dangerous, like getting drowned.'" Then they would design and build their rafts, their own tugs and freighters, and haul rocks and lumber up and down in their private river world. The fever never left them.

And adding to that seductive call, the sternwheeler *Weown* would occasionally lay along the face of the dock, waiting out a storm. The boys, always hungry, would scramble aboard, win the hearts of the crew, and beg a huge sandwich, which was always generously given.

"Someday, I'll work on one of these," each boy was dreaming. Well, those grand, old steam vessels had given way to the diesel tugs by the time the boys were old enough to be captains, but captains they did become. The younger boy became a superb mechanic, and loved his engines; but in the latter half of his career the bridge won out over the engine room, and he became one of the most highly respected and skilled tugboatmen on the Columbia.

The kid, too, had divided loyalties; the airplane and its magic wings also called, and he spent some years in air traffic control in Alaska. But he kept his seamanship alive with sailboats, and motor boats, and an occasional boat job, so that the skills never really faded away.

But we're getting away; let us return to the kid on the river.

Far from being all romance and adventure, life at sea on a small boat can mean long, long hours of weary toil and empty, yet full in their peculiar way, day upon day of infinite loneliness. Yet I find that the weariness is proof for that inner need to know that I have earned my pay, and the loneliness becomes the glass through which I see my life, the frame for the picture of my life, the necessary backdrop for the drama of my life; the illumination for the way of my life.

Because I Must

> I'm alone on my ship as the salt sprays fly,
> and the scattered clouds grace a clear, blue sky,
> and a lonely eagle shares my cry,
> as he rules his winged throne on high,
> that this we know we must do or die.
> I'll never know if the tireless sea
> can be as lonely for him as it can for me,
> or if weary hours dragging endlessly
> or if aching bones or back can be

Kid on the River

the price he knows he pays to be free.
But I know the price when a long, long run
has kept us going from sun to sun
and my limbs grow weary 'ere the harbor's won,
and I feel all the loneliness of one
who knows he must sail till his life is done.
The blessing of life is toil, they say,
and my worn frame tells that I surely pay.
But the lonely hours are the searching ray
that frames my life, that lights the way,
and I know why I sail on the sea this day.
November 30, 1965

From the book, *Islands of Experience*, by the same author

Chapter 6
Knute

A Tug Company Is Born

As most older ones will remember, "times were tough" in the late '20s. But the unique resourcefulness of the kid's dad always found a way. That taste of the waters that was awakened in him never left. That strong flow of Indian blood in his veins gave him a vision of the horizons; but his blood and heritage of sea captains from Deer Isle, Maine, also called.

One day he found himself towing logs at a most unlikely place, Northwestern Lake, north of White Salmon, Washington. But an opportunity came to bid on a gravel hauling job, back on the Columbia. The State of Washington was building a new highway near Lyle and needed several thousand yards of gravel. So he convinced the gravel plant of Lofts and Son at Hood River to bid on the supply. Together they bid, and won the supply and delivery contract.

But now the vision had to be made into reality. He traded the small motorboat, with which he'd been towing logs on Northwestern Lake, for the bare 25- to 30-foot hull of an old, riveted steel, double-ended lifeboat. Somewhere he found a four-cylinder, 45 hp gasoline, Holt tractor engine and a Mack truck transmission, and put them all together to create his first real towboat. I even believe I know the diameter and pitch of that first propeller; it was a 28x20.

Luke Nichols Towing Company first Tug, a 25 to 30 foot, riveted steel lifeboat.

But the whole contraption worked. One had but to step on the clutch, shift the transmission into high gear, and you were direct drive ahead. Reverse, however, was a little short. But, as I said, it worked.

Next was the barge. With his skills at dickering and dealing, he went to Portland and bought an old, but serviceable, wooden barge, for $200 and had it delivered to the landing at the foot of the Dock Road. That was the narrow, very steep road that had been built so many years before to link the town to their dock, and their only transportation link with the rest of the world. As we earlier said, the sternwheeler *Weown* was still making runs on the river and was probably the one to deliver the barge.

With no winches, and probably not even cleats on that wobbly hull, they were really unable to make up to the barge, so they towed it on a long towline. The head (toilet) was over the side, and cooking was done over a bonfire on one of the gravel piles on the barge.

And now we hear about Knute. Actually, I believe his first name was Ernest, and his last name Knute. But everyone, even the boys, just called him Knute. He had drifted in from the hobo jungles one day, and attached himself, for the rest of his life, to the kid's dad. Although he nipped at the wine bottle whenever he could, he was not really a "wino." He had had great tragedy in his life, had lost his way, and so clung to his new employer as a servant to a master. But it was an arrangement that served them both well until Knute's death, 15 to 20 years later. He was never paid a salary, but lived free in an old floathouse at one of the logbooms. Whenever he needed a few dollars for groceries, or a rare piece of clothing, he just asked for $5 or $10. He really had few urgent needs except the need to belong. And over the years, he became a counselor, a sort of Godfather, to the kid and his younger brother.

I don't know that he was much of a mechanic, but having served some years aboard real sailing ships, and then some years as a hobo, he could do almost anything else, such as carpentry, and, back to the bonfire on the gravel pile, he could really cook up a meal. Whether in a hobo jungle, or on a gravel pile on a barge in the middle of the Columbia River, a bonfire is a bonfire; the ship's cook was at home in his "galley." Of course, young boys are always hungry, and just maybe those meals were not all that outstanding, but 50 years later those two boys still smile at the tasty memories of those eggs, and bacon, and hotcakes covered with the delightful flavor of burnt-sugar syrup.

I mentioned earlier, that "wobbly" hull. I don't think it had ribs at all—just a couple of thwarts or so, no decks, and certainly no house at all—so it wobbled in harmony with that old "Cat" engine. After all, the ribs and decks don't tow barges; engines and propellers do. But Knute's talents began to emerge. On those long, slow hauls up the river to Lyle, Washington, he began fitting in ribs, and decking, and cabin, and making a tugboat out of his steel, eggshell hull.

Knute was a little slow, and I don't think he was very strong, although he seemed always there, working at something, whether rafting logs, boring boomsticks, or rebuilding a small barge that had come floating down the river one day. So he probably didn't help with the initial techniques for unloading that gravel. A strong, young man by the name of Henry "Hank" Troh had joined the Company, and for a while, he and that powerful tugboat captain filled the arriving gravel trucks by hand, shoveling that gravel into them with huge scoop shovels. Knute, however, helped build a hopper and a small donkey, and then ran the donkey, which pulled a "Fresno" scoop full of gravel up into the hopper. The strong, young men guided that Fresno. It was still hard work, but it was much faster. The trucks had now only to back under the hopper and be filled in seconds.

A Sailing Barge

Knute built the kid a sailboat. Well, it didn't start out that way. As detailed more in the next chapter, the kid's dad had contracted, a few years later, to haul logs by truck around the incomplete Bonneville Locks. Their base camp was on Bradford Island, the base also for much of the continuing construction of the Dam.

Around any construction project there is always a residue of building materials, leftovers from this or that interim project. At the logboom where they were lifting the logs from the water, they had need for a small, tough boat, into which they could throw heavy boomchains, peaveys, axes, and wire swifters. So Knute built one.

He sent the two boys out to "scrounge" some twoinch planks. They came back with a number of 2x6s, 2x8s, 2xl0s, and 2xl2s. But they had also found a 24-foot 2xl6. It was an unusual dimension, but ideal for the sides of the boat, or barge, Knute planned to build. The old sailorcarpenter went to work. The barge would be 4 feet wide, and 12 feet long. The skills of this quiet man emerged even more.

He cut all the bottom pieces, with their varying widths, at exactly four feet each, and then planed off the edge of each one, just a bit, so that there would be an open slot, half way in, between each plank. He could then later drive in the oakum for calking the seams, making them water tight.

Knute

Although this was really just a tough, floating box, it just could not look like that, so on each end Knute cut the sideboards, for eight inches, at an angle of 45 degrees, then vertically on to the top. A 2x8 covered that angle, and another, the last eight inches vertically. They had a rough but good-looking barge, even with rakes. Oarlocks on the gunnels, and a seat nailed across near the middle, and one on the stern, and a very useful little boat was complete. No one thought of painting.

One day, the kid said to Knute, "I wish I had a sailboat."

And Knute answered simply, "Well, we can make one out of that little scow. Here's what we'll do. We'll build a gaff rig, using a piece of that old, brown canvas. You go out in the woods and find me three fir saplings, and strip the bark. We'll need one about 15 feet long for the mast, one about 10 feet long for the boom, and a smaller one, about 12 feet long for the gaff."

The kid scurried out for the saplings; Knute cut the sail, nailed a piece of 2x8 on the sole, and another across, on top the gunnels. Each had a hole for stepping the mast; an oarlock was set in the stern; an oar would serve as rudder.

"We can't install a keel, or centerboard," Knute observed, "So we'll have to have leeboards," and explained about what he thought they needed. So the kid found a smooth, 1x12, and cut two, three-foot pieces, even planning the leading and trailing edges to streamline them. He bolted the center of each leeboard to each side of the barge, with half-inch bolts, and then thought, "If I don't want to be taking those leeboards off and on, I can bore two more half-inch holes off to one side, and use another bolt just as a pin to hold the board either down for sailing, or up alongside the hull at all other times." It worked perfectly.

This was to be the simplest of simple rigs. There would be no halyard. Knute simply tied, with quarter-inch rope, the boom and the gaff to the mast, about a foot above the thwart through which the mast was stepped, and tied the four corners of the sail to the mast, boom, and gaff with more quarter-inch rope. A single length of one-quarter served as main sheet. The boat was ready to sail. To dowse the sail, one had only to lift the boom, catch the gaff on the way up, and gather both to the mast, with the sail, lift the assemblage from the step, and lay it down. Hoisting sail was as simple.

There was so little wind at Bonneville that sailing there escapes memory. But a short time later, they were back at White Salmon, with the west winds of the Columbia Gorge. And there he found that that little ship really sailed. Making perhaps as much as 4 knots, in a broad reach, in 25-knot winds, he and his big, German shepherd dog sailed across that mile-wide river, up its broad course, and down its stormy width. When that flat bottom came off those huge, six- to eight-foot waves (they have been measured at over 22 feet), and struck the water again with thunder, the legs of that shepherd, standing in the bow, would quiver like steel springs; but he stayed right there. And the young captain laughed, and yelled, and sailed for more.

Tugboats called the young captain, and that little sailboat drifted into memory. But a seed was planted in the heart of a boy with the heritage of the sea in his veins. It would never die. A lovely, nostalgic memory of a simple but very real sailboat, and old Knute who created her, remains.

Knute was a mystery, perhaps one might say an enigma, and some might call him just an old wino, a failure in life. But the two boys who grew into their own towboat careers, guided not a little by this quiet man, remember him always, with a tear not far from the edges of their eyes. Don't speak evil of old Knute around them.

Chapter 7
Slim

The building of Bonneville Dam greatly reshaped, physically, economically, and even spiritually, the flow of history on the mid-Columbia. And the kid was being molded too by that history-making event.

For a year or so, several months at least, the water level above the dam had been reached, but the locks were not yet ready for traffic; so the tugboat men had to innovate. The kid's dad contracted with loggers and sawmills, to haul their logs out of the water just above the powerhouse, haul them by truck around to the estuary below, and re-raft them. The kid was boomcat, hooking the tongs and slings for lifting out the logs, and his younger brother ran the Donkey. And both boys ran the boomboat, jockeying rafts around. Old Knute cooked on the tiny crew-quarters barge (no gravel piles this time) and did the many odd jobs always around.

It was there that Knute built the 4-foot by 12-foot barge out of scavenged two-inch planks, and at the kid's cry, converted to that sailboat. It was there that the kid watched yet another history-making event, as the innovative tug, the *Mary Gail*, pushed the first, small bargeload (about 75,000 gallons, I believe) of gasoline from Bonneville up the river, and even on beyond the Celilo Falls and Canal before The Dalles Dam was built. Since the locks were not yet in operation, the fuel was brought up river to the lower side by barges, and pumped through to the waiting barges on the upper side.

And it was there that the kid watched still another birth of industry, as the new river tanker, the *Inland Chief*, brought fuel to the lower side of the dam, to be also pumped to her waiting barges on the upper side. The *Inland Chief* was a fine ship, but tying up those big engines and crew for the long pumping process was not sound economics; so the Company later cut her into two pieces and made out of her a tug and a barge. *Inland Navigation* was born.

And it was about that time that Capt. "Slim" Leppaluoto brought his two tugs, the *Robert Gray*, with her 100 hp CO (for crude oil), Fairbanks Morse engine, and the tug, *Mystic*, down from Grays Harbor. For a time Slim worked closely with the kid's dad, and won not only the very real respect of all, but their affection as well.

In reference to that respect, one very dark night they had just landed a raft of logs against the steep bank of Eagle Creek, a half mile or so up the estuary from the powerhouse. The kid was up in the brush securing the end of a swifter line that would hold the raft there. He had run out of "mousing," the small cords from unraveled larger rope, that they used to secure the ends of the knotted chains on the swifter ends. So he hollered down through the night, "Somebody bring me some mousing."

Instead of the familiar voice of his dad, agreeing to the request, the unmistakable voice of Captain Slim Leppaluoto bellowed back through the darkness, "Come and get your own mousing." The kid learned a real lesson in respect that night; and, he never found himself without a pocket full of mousing after that either.

But there were other things about Slim, as those close to him dared to call him, that won respect. One time, that wild, west wind had not let up, day or night, for over two weeks. The kid's dad owned the Underwood Log Dump and boom, and had a contract to deliver piling to the dam. But one could not tow a log raft in those terrible swells, and a raft of piling would not last half a mile.

Slim

In desperation the engineers at the dam called and said, "Damn the cost, we'll pay by the hour; bring us piling if you have to bring them one at a time."

So Slim said, "I can get them there." They took 10 or 15 piling, and laced a dogline over and under, over and under, across the head, *and* tail of that tiny raft. A "dogline" is a piece of one-half to five-eighths inch wire rope, with "dogs" strung on the wire. The "dog" was a piece of steel with a ring on one end through which the wire ran; the other end was wedge shaped for driving into the logs. Its wedge shape also allowed for knocking them back out later with a sideways blow from a "dog axe." A dog was driven into every piling.

When the raft was ready, and with the kid's younger brother as deckhand, Captain Slim started out, probably with the *Mystic*, down that wild river. It was 22 feet from the water to the top of the light mast on that small tug, yet as the shore crew watched, the entire boat, mast and all, would disappear in the hollow of those huge swells. But Slim delivered his piling to Bonneville, and the construction of Bonneville Dam continued on.

But towing logs was too slow for the driving energy of this tall Finn. So he went on to barging, and the beginning of a whole, new towing industry, barging gasoline and other

petroleum products up the river. He later became head of Inland Navigation Company, headquartered in The Dalles, one of the two major barge towing companies on the mid- and upper-Columbia.

But Slim never lost his humanity. Nearly 20 years after the kid learned his first lesson in respect for this great man, the kid and his wife, were struck head-on by a careless, young soldier on the highway east of The Dalles. For the week or two that they were in the hospital there, I don't think Slim and his wife missed a day coming to visit them. Yes, Slim, I think that, even today, if you bellowed at the kid to "Come and get your own mousing," he would leap into action, and do it with a great big grin on his face.

Kid on the River

The new Nichols 38 foot tug, *Louise N.*, being lifted over the incomplete Bonneville Dam locks, October 14, 1937.

Chapter 8

Bridge of the Gods

The kid knew he would one day captain the tugs. There were to be hard times, bitter times, incredibly wearying times, but always the washing waters of that great waterway, ever stirred by the western winds, called, and called.

Increasingly, the summer months of his high school days were spent on the water, rafting logs, running boom boats, and decking on the tugs.

One day, with his older brother-in-law, Jack, at the wheel of the newest Company tug, they were making the sharp "S" turn in the river between the now-covered Cascade Rapids, and the new steel Bridge of the Gods. The three log rafts followed as the skilled, young captain twisted and turned them around those rocky curves. The kid stood out on the after deck and mentally calculated how he himself would have made those turns. He would not have made them the same, but he would have made them. He knew he was ready; and in less time than his memory can recall, he was, indeed, captain of that small ship.

But as he stood out on that after deck, watching the turbulent water troubling the tug and her tow, he thought about the old Indian legends of how those rapids had been formed. "The gods had built," the legend said, "a stone bridge across the great river there. It was so massive, there was even a small forest of trees growing on its stony deck. One day the gods grew angry, and shook the earth, and the Bridge of the Gods fell into the river, damming, for a short while, the flow of the water. But as the water rose and flowed over the dam, a roaring rapids now marked the grave of that bridge and her small forest."

A year or so before Bonneville Dam was completed, the kid's other brother-in-law, Lloyd, was running a small tug there. He was tending a drill rig that had been anchored out over the lip of those rapids to drill and blast apart some of the larger boulders so that they would not interfere with the desired channel depth when the dam was completed.

It was an unusual position to be in; and as they looked down into the clear water, they saw a standing forest of trees. Oh, most of the limbs were torn off, but they were definitely standing trees. "No, they were not deadheads (sunken logs) that had jammed there, I tell you, they were standing trees," the men had insisted.

And the kid remembered something else. Before the dam was built, and one time when the river was very low, he had been running one of the boomboats back up the river on a very dark night. He had gotten too close to the Oregon shore, somewhere east of the Cascade Locks. When he snapped on his searchlight, he was in a small forest of jagged stumps of long-dead trees. They had obviously died in the distant past when "something" had raised, forever, the level of the river. There is much geologic evidence that the natural damming of the river at the Cascades was very sudden.

The kid was part of history now. But something called from that distant past, and cried, that for him, that past was not so distant at all.

Chapter 9
The Corbett Light

With their heavy rafts of logs of such varying sizes that it seemed every log dug its heels into the water, the little tugs were plodding work horses, dragging down a slow-moving river. But as anyone knows, time has flown, since time began. And again, in less time than memory can recall, the kid was indeed signed on as captain of a documented vessel on a federal stream.

For a couple of years or so, the kid's principal job was towing logs from the Company log boom at Underwood, Washington, to Portland and Vancouver. Usually he took three rafts at a time, totaling one-quarter to one-half of a million board feet. And he became quietly proud of his ability to take three rafts to Portland, and return the tug home in 60 running hours without shutting the engine down except for refueling at the oil dock.

And about this time, another small event passed that lifted this budding young captain's self-esteem. The Bonneville Locks were 75 feet wide and 500 feet long. So, the rafts were built about 70 feet wide, and 490 plus feet long. Obviously, they were locked through one at a time. But it also meant that with a three-raft tow, on one round trip to the Portland area, the kid made six passages through the locks.

Curiously, in those days, the "trip number" on the passage manifest for the lock authorities was recorded as the captain's own trip number. It was later changed, of course, because captains changed, and it made better sense to record the vessel's "trip number." But it was not so in the beginning.

One dark, rainy night (it almost always rained at Bonneville), the kid recorded "trip number 500," and sent the manifest up on the cord the lock tender had dropped down. Sometime later, the lock tender called down into that concrete canyon, "Captain, do you realize, you are the first to make 500 trips through these locks?"

No, the kid had not thought about it, because he knew that the oil barge tugs made more trips up the river than he did. But when they made a round trip, that meant only two passages through the locks. When the kid made a round trip, it meant, usually, six passages. The numbers had added up. A dubious honor, perhaps, and certainly not a major, historic event. But, in a tiny way the kid had indeed made history, back there in the year of 1939.

Most budding companies in those days "operated on a shoestring." Certainly this one did. So there was little money to pay deckhands who could stay long enough to learn the river. They often took along friends, or school chums who, though they could steer some in the daylight, were almost helpless at night. As a result, the kid had to steer part or most of the day, and nearly all of the night. After a while, coffee just didn't work anymore, and he soon found that he could fall asleep while sitting up on the stool at the wheel. For many hours, of many nights, he stood up at the wheel, so that if he fell asleep, he would fall to the deck and be sharply re-awakened.

One clear night, with a couple of old school buddies aboard, he had just cleared Cape Horn. Ahead was perhaps an hour or more straight run, angling down and across the river to the Tunnel Point Light, a bright, flashing white light near Corbett, and so was often called the Corbett Light.

"I've just got to get some sleep, fellas," the kid told them. "See that flashing white light?; take you an hour or so to get there. When you do, hold a little to the right of it, and wake me up."

The Corbett Light

In seconds, the kid was sound asleep on the wheelhouse bunk. An hour or so later, but in what seemed to the kid like only seconds later, the boys woke him up.

"Where do we go now, Cap?" they asked.

The kid, dazed with sleep, raised up on an elbow, looked out the forward windows and said, "See that flashing white light down there? Steer a little to the right of it, and wake me when you get there."

Again, time for him had no meaning. But when he was awakened the next time, it was not by his novice, though eager helpers; it was by the special feel and sound of a boat in shallow water. The Venturi principle was at work. The boat was, to use the unpoetic term of the river, sucking down.

A semi-tunnel stern boat, as this one was, is worse, because the propeller is also speeding up the water, but even a loaded barge will "suck down" in shallow water, as much as a foot or more. The flow of water, because of the restricted space between the stream bottom and the bottom of the vessel, speeds up, and the Venturi principle, "pressure is least where speed is greatest," goes to work, so decreasing the pressure on the bottom of the vessel that it literally falls to the bottom and bumps along.

It took a few moments for the kid to look around and put it all together; they were running up on the upper, Oregon edge of that Sandy River bar. He hollered at the boys to take in the towline as he backed full to get away. Finally able to turn, he swung around the raft that was still charging down on them, caught the towline tight, and poured on the power. The logs, not drawing as much water, never grounded, but slowly turned and followed back into deeper water and onto their next course for the Washougal Dolphin.

But what had happened? Well, the novices had made no mistakes, at least that were their fault. And in a way, neither had the kid. There is a flashing, white light marking the end of a short jetty just as the Sandy Bar starts to turn the Columbia north. If its time and interval are not exactly the same as the Tunnel Point Light, it is, or was, very close.

It was such a clear night that when the boys had reached the Tunnel Point Light, they just held off shore a fair distance and passed the light by a thousand feet or so, and then woke the kid. And he, thinking he had not really been asleep at all, looked out the forward windows, saw the Gary Island Light, and, thinking it was just the Tunnel Point Light, repeated his instructions.

Although this was not at all a matter of life and death, it is quite clear that the kid's Guardian Angel had done some work for him, again, this night, back there in the year 1939.

Chapter 10

Lost Love
and Lesson Learned

I suppose that one might deduce, from reading these stories, that all was chaos and trouble on the tugs. Of course it was not that. Those were the things that make for stories. Most of the long, steady hours were a gentle, pleasant ride down a strikingly beautiful river, between magnificent mountains standing so tall on either side that often they pierced the gentle clouds and made them cry. And those tears of heaven would gather in the crags, and here and there the high, stony walls would spill them out in a waterfall so tall, that the winds would often whip them into white, feathery plumes.

Sunrises and sunsets of indescribable beauty were often there, seemingly for the tugboatmen alone, turning the loneliness of those dark hours into quiet gifts from God. No, clearly, all was not chaos and trouble on the tugs.

And there were funny things that happened too. This was a very typical, tiny tug, with her decks built low to the water for working close to the logs she towed. Her wheelhouse overhead (roof) extended back over the engine house just far enough for a full-size, spring-filled mattress to lay there.

In a recess under the bunk, a tiny stove was bolted down. It was well named, a "Chummy." Ten inches in diameter, and 12

33

inches high, it was designed to burn what were then called Gasco briquettes. I think they have not been available for years now, but then they were an ideal solid fuel. They burned like coal, but with no ash at all. With its smoke pipe running up the stack beside the engine exhaust pipe, that little stove made a neat, compact heating system, and filled with briquettes, it would hold a steady fire for over 10 hours. The cabin was always snug and warm.

Slats across the underside of the overhead joists held an assortment of magazines; up in one corner, a radio kept the very real music of those times, Tommy Dorsey and Guy Lombardo, overriding the comforting throb of the engine; and just aft of the engine room, a tiny galley held a Coleman gas stove, an icebox, and the best of foods for an always-hungry crew. Could a luxury yacht really have more of these essentials? Oh, it could have them in more polished form, but in off times the boys found that the girls would readily go "cruising" on the river with them, on their tugboat yachts.

In fact, it was on one such moonlight cruise that the kid discovered a very useful fact about his new, Atlas diesel engine. The troublesome Buda had been replaced with the heavier-duty Atlas. But the Atlas was air starting; that is, a tank of compressed air was kept charged. With an exposed, massive flywheel, the engine, according to instructions, was "barred over" to "starting position" by inserting a bar in one of the holes in the rim of that flywheel and turning the crankshaft to that position. The main air valve was turned on, and then the "starting lever" was thrown over, engaging the cams in their proper sequence that lifted the normally closed starting valves. For a few moments, some of the cylinders worked, in their turn, as an air motor, and the others as a diesel engine. It always started, but it was a somewhat slow and cumbersome process, especially that barring over to "starting position."

On this night cruise of learning, the kid had taken his girl up the river as far as the Hood River–White Salmon bridge; and, since there was no wind at all, shut the engine down for a quiet drift down the river. He had left his running lights on. He knew that that was technically illegal, but, he reasoned, it was better than

Lost Love and Lesson Learned

no lights at all. And besides, with so little traffic on the river then, probably, no one would notice anyway.

But somehow, time gets lost when a young man is with a young girl in a warm cabin, on a peaceful river, with soft music playing. They had drifted down opposite the White Salmon River. The cold air from Mt. Adams that, on the still nights, flowed down the canyon of the White Salmon along with the river, had the drifting tug almost into the willows on the Oregon side. Aroused from their concentration by shouting voices, they looked out to see a flashlight in someone's hand, bouncing toward them only yards away.

The kid dove for the engine room in minor panic. He was not so fearful of running aground; he just couldn't imagine how he would explain things to his "rescuers." In a rush, and with practiced skill, he turned on the air valve and threw the starting lever over, demanding that the engine start without that "barring over" procedure. It started readily.

And from that day onward, he *never* again bothered to "bar the engine over" for starting.

Curious, isn't it, that nearly 50 years later his memory would recall the details of that corrected starting procedure, but not the name of the girl who had lured him out upon the river that night.

Chapter 11

Breakdown at Hamilton Island

We have mentioned that Buda diesel engine, the original engine in the kid's first tug. Buda builds fine engines, just like Chevrolet, Ford, and Chrysler build fine cars. But like those big three, once in a while they have a bad one. That Buda was one. And trouble it gave. Like the time, landing a log raft against Hamilton Island, just around the first bend below the Bonneville Locks.

Right in against the gravelly shore, the water was nearly slack, but of course a raft would not stay there. The kid had just completed the landing and backed up to catch a towline on an outer joint, so that he could pull ahead and in, to place the raft snug against the shore while his deckhand secured the line that ran down from a tree higher on the bank. When he again shifted the transmission (called a reverse gear on a tug) ahead, the propeller did not turn. The engine ran, but the propeller would not turn. The shifting forks inside the gear box had broken, and would not engage the forward clutch. Time stood still, for a few moments, but only for a few. The raft and the disabled tug would obviously soon go drifting down that swiftly flowing stream, surely to crash on rocks below.

Most of the reverse gears on the early tugs worked in a refined way perhaps, but they worked much like the old Model T car. There was no literal shifting of gears. For forward, there was a disc clutch to engage the engine shaft straight through to the propeller shaft. It was the forks on this clutch that had broken. But, like the old Model T, the reverse worked by applying, literally, a brake to the reverse drum, forcing the "planetary" gears inside the drum to turn the propeller shaft in the opposite direction.

The kid tried his reverse. It worked fine. Though small, this was a new and modern tug with "monkey rudders," small rudders above and below the propeller shaft, and just ahead of the propeller. They gave excellent steering in reverse. So he backed out into the river in a circle, came back in along the forward end of the raft, caught a hookline, and, backing full, pulled the raft up the necessary 100 feet or so, and then jammed it against the gravel so the deckhand could secure it to the shore. The day was ruined, but the tow and tug were saved.

Curiously again, though memory recalls these vivid details, it does not recall how they got news home. But probably a passing tug, some hours later, saw their distress signal, and carried the news to the nearest phone at the locks, and a mechanic was brought down to effect the repairs.

That Buda was a problem, but a boy captain matured some that day.

OUR OWN

The fog hangs low and drifting, drifting swiftly on the breeze;
the sky peeks through and spreads its blue for a moment on the sea.
The wavelets ring their tinkling bells against the hull,
and from the sky comes the hungry cry of a lonely, gliding gull.

* * * *

Two pursers hang on slanting scopes of anchor line.
The cluster of small boats attached speaks well of wine,
but friendship too and sharing of tall tales
of bigger hauls and thicker fogs and gales.

* * * *

Kid on the River

The flooding tide so soon will hide the sand surrounding us, and then will be but a tiny sea with a wall of mist, and thus three tiny ships will find themselves at anchor and all alone, in a world that I, with the mist and the sky and solitude, call our own.

Aboard the *M/V Brant*

Kanak Island, Alaska

September 9, 1965

From the book, *Islands of Experience*

by the same author.

Chapter 12

Victory at Hamilton Island

Sometimes shortcuts, coupled with diversions, cause problems. It had been a good day. The kid and his deckhand, an older man named George, had two rafts for Portland, one for one mill, and one for another. Before locking through at Bonneville, it didn't make any difference which one was ahead; but the delivery would be more easily effected with the number two raft ahead.

They had locked the first raft through and taken it the mile down river, and secured it to their tieline along the gravel beach of Hamilton Island. When they arrived hours later with the number two raft, they swung it in just upstream of the first raft. In order to swing the rafts out of that fast water into the semi-slack water against the island, they had to turn them in a big circle, leaving them again headed upstream.

The log rafts have a long boomstick across the tail end called, curiously, the header. On the forward end, or peak, the two side sticks are drawn together about 45 degrees each, making a point out of the lead end. With the second raft now the lead raft, a boom-chain was "choked" around the middle of its header, and coupled to the peak of the first raft, still secured to the shore. It was their intention to quickly cut loose the first raft, hook a towline onto the outer corner of its header, and haul the two rafts out into the current and down the river backwards a few miles to opposite Butler's Eddy, or Dent's Boom, as some called it. There, the fast water ended; the Columbia was again a slow-moving stream, ambling to the sea. They could turn their tow around in their own time.

But sometimes, shortcuts, coupled with diversions and small problems, cause big problems. When they arrived with the second raft, they found the kid's father-in-law and a buddy fishing for sturgeon off the anchored raft. That in itself was no problem, but the ensuing conversation diverted the kid's attention. And, old George was having trouble getting the shoreline free. It all took more time than "Plan A" had allowed for. When the kid glanced up the rafts, he was shocked to see that the peak of the lead raft was swinging out into the swift current. It was already out 25 or 30 degrees. If it went past 45 degrees, the bind against the peak of the lower raft would most likely break its header in two, spilling loose logs all over the river.

The kid yelled at the struggling George, "Get that line loose and c'mon." George's adrenalin must have responded to the driving urgency in his young captain's voice, for somehow he found the strength to clear the line and run for the tug.

The kid's mind was racing. They had never turned *two* rafts around there; the river was not much over 1,200 feet wide, and each raft was 490 feet long. It was too late to grab the trailing raft and get it moving before that lead raft came around that 15 to 25 degrees more that would surely mean destruction. So he dashed for the first or second joint back on that lead raft, nosed the tug in there, and poured on the power, slowing the swing, but also pushing the raft out into the river. The trailing raft followed.

Again, time seemed to stand still as the battle raged. But the buckling of the lead raft against the trailing one had been stopped; the whole of a quarter of a million board feet of logs, and a tiny tug, turned in a great circle down and toward the cliffs of the Oregon shore.

A hundred feet before they reached those jagged rocks, the kid figured he might have it made, backed off and ran to the peak. George hooked on the towline, and the kid opened the engine to full ahead. Slowly the two rafts straightened out behind him, barely a thousand feet above a rocky island on the Washington side.

Only then did the kid start breathing freely again. And then he thought about his father-in-law and his friend. "My God, George," he exclaimed, "what happened to those fishermen?"

"Oh, when they heard you yell," George grinned, "and we ran for the peak of that raft, I looked back and saw two scared fishermen grabbing their gear and running for the shore. Oh, they made it alright."

There is no question that the whole battle was a real victory that day, but sometimes shortcuts do cause problems.

Chapter 13

Audacity- or Daring?

As we recall these stories, we may bounce around a bit, that is, from the kid's very novice days to his skilled and mature days and back again. And sometimes, we may share a story of his in-between days where his skills were definitely emerging, yet where the brashness of youth gave him a certain audacity that crowded his credit with his "Special Loan Program," as administered by his Guardian Angel. This is a story of one of those days, or, in this case, one of those nights.

During low flows of the Columbia, the boys had found that they could haul all three rafts at one time out of the still estuary below the locks, and into the fast water of the main stream, and, although it was always close, hold them off the rocks on the outside of that curve a half mile down. So, though they still had to lock the rafts through one at a time, they could make up their three-raft tow in that quiet estuary, rather than take the hour or two to Hamilton Island, and back for each raft, or worse, the two to four hours to take each one to Butler's Eddy, five miles downriver, to make up the three-raft tow.

The kid was just coming out of the locks with his third raft, and met one of the Smith tugs upriver bound. They had seen his two rafts already through, and his third coming out.

Audacity- or Daring?

"You'll never make it, Cap," they called over, "The b_____s have cut away the island on the upper side. The main river current cuts smack into the shore right at the corner now."

The kid thanked the Smith tug, who ran on into the locks, and then he finished moving his own raft into position to complete his tow. Then he ran out to the river, in the darkness, to look the situation over with his searchlight. The "situation" was as the Smith tug had said. The 1,000 feet or so that they used to have, where the slack water paralleled the racing current, and where they could ease their sluggish tows into that current and pick up its speed—that 1,000 feet was gone. The slack water butted at 90 degrees directly into the current. At first glance, an impossible situation.

The U.S. Army Corp of Engineers, like the U.S. Coast Guard, enjoys a certain amount of earned respect from the seamen on the water, because, unlike most government agencies, they usually did a pretty good job and they usually had the interests of the tugs in mind, as well as that of the other users of the river's power. But this time some engineer had failed to do all of his engineering.

Probably they had cut the island back to give a bit better exhaust to the powerhouse tailrace; but whatever the reason, it was clearly unrelated to improved navigation.

Well, enough of bitterness; what to do now? The kid had, of course, inherited his dad's capacity to think on his feet. So he set to thinking. The locks were being filled to lift that Smith tug to the upper level. When full, that huge chamber held nearly two million cubic feet of water. That was a lot of water, and as it was released from the locks on lowering, it would, the kid reasoned, just have to push that line, between the slack water and the racing current, further out. The water coming out would not be fast, but it should be just enough boost to shove them out to safety.

So he climbed up the stairs to present the challenge to the lock tender. "Sure," the lock tender said, "It's kind of a dull night anyway, let's see if it will work."

"Now hold the water until I give you a long blast on my whistle," the kid instructed. "I don't want it too soon, or too late."

"OK, Cap, we'll do it," he answered.

And now that marvelous part of the human mind that calculates the unknowable started racing in his head. Exactly how long does it take to tow that 1,200 feet or so out to the river? How long does it take for the massive valves to be opened after the lock tender hears the whistle? And how long will it take for that slow flow to reach him and his heavy rafts?

In retrospect, I think this may not at all have been a case of crowding his "Special Loan Program." This may not at all have been a case of brashness, but rather one of calculated daring, where the kid had put every fiber, every ounce of his accumulated skill and knowledge on the line. And the Holy Spirit, through his Guardian Angel, picked up the challenge with delight.

The deckhand cut the tow loose; they hooked on the towline and poured on full power, every log, as always, dragging its heels in resistance. They had a short towline for better control; the searchlight flashed ahead seeking the edge of that swift water. Yet the kid looked around, not really looking, but more like a quarterback, listening with his spirit for the right timing, and the right signal to call.

Now! His whistle sounded its long blast, and died away. Nothing happened. Had the lock man changed his mind? Maybe he didn't hear? Was there trouble with the valves? The searchlight pierced the darkness .There, 500 feet out, the menacing edge of the slicing river. The rafts were following, swiftly now, it seemed. A few more minutes, and they would be committed.

The deckhand, out on the after deck, was watching closely for the boiling water to begin below the lock gate. There, it was beginning.

"It's coming, Cap, it's coming," he shouted. But the flow was not reaching them yet. The searchlight showed the racing river only 200 feet away now, and off to the left, still striking the shore right at the corner. Minutes passed. The nose of the tug was only feet from the river now; they were committed.

But look, the searchlight swung to that corner; the river was being forced out—slowly, slowly, the margin widened. The tug and tow picked up speed, just a little, as that two million cubic feet of water told the mighty Columbia, "Move over, this tug and tow and daring young captain and I are coming out." And come out they did, with not a scratch against that southern shore.

Brashness, or audacity, or daring? Well, call it what you will, but I think a special Guardian Angel smiled on a daring, young tugboat captain that night.

Chapter 14
Bonneville Again

Courage

The kid's dad was such a physical and emotional giant, he was really incapable of seeing his two sons as mere boys. It was low flow time on the Columbia, but they had a three-raft tow to take out of Bonneville. This was perhaps a year before that previous, island-cut-away event. The kid was really a novice. They had two tugs for the extra push they felt they needed, but if the kid was a novice, his brother, two years younger, and still a high school student, was greener still.

Though of course, he later went on to be one of the best tug skippers on the river, that day he was a frightened boy, and told his older brother so. "I can't do it, brother, I just can't," he pleaded. Well, the kid was scared too, but an older brother couldn't admit it at a time like that, so he learned another lesson in maturity as he talked up the courage of another boy captain, and convinced him that he *could* do it. Then they planned their maneuvers and hauled those rafts out and down the river.

Sometimes one wonders why so much pain is required to teach us the lessons of life and maturity.

Bonneville Again

The View . . .

But funny things happened at Bonneville too. Every so often, the U.S. Army Corp of Engineers launch, *Sandy*, would lock through with them. The kid had noted that the operator, as soon as his boat was secured, would always jump up on his wheelhouse bunk with his binoculars in his hand.

One day, the two boats were close enough so that the kid could step over and ask, "OK, what's this binocular routine about?"

"Oh, it's the view, man, it's the view."

They were settling down into a concrete, vertical walled canyon. The view?

"Yeah man, take a look at that one with the white skirt."

The view, yes. That was in the days when girls still wore skirts, full skirts, and the breezes, swirling around those walls did marvelous things. Young men noticed those marvelous things.

History?

On the bright, sunny days—yes, I know I said it always rained at Bonneville, but it didn't always rain, it *almost* always rained; when the sun shone, it was glorious —but on the bright, sunny days, especially on weekends, tourists lined the rails above, watching the locking through process.

To add some spice to the long runs up the river, the boys had built a surfboard." At least, that's what they called it. It was probably the forerunner of water skis. But it was quite different. A single board about two feet wide and five feet long, it had a small towline attached to its underside, running to the tug. And on the upper side, a rope bridle looped back for the rider to hold. It gave marvelous stability and marvelous control; and although those old tugs barely made 12 mph or so, still, they had some good "surfboarding" on the long runs home.

One day, the kid had been riding the board up through the fast water below the locks, on a sunny, Sunday afternoon. As they rounded the corner into the lock canal, they saw that the gates were open, and there was a crowd of tourists at the rails. The kid couldn't resist the temptation and waved the helmsman on into the locks. There was really no unusual danger, but it did look a bit spectacular, whether the tourists were impressed or not.

The lock tender was not.

When the tug reached the upper level, he summoned the kid, captain of a tugboat, mind you, up to his operator's room, and rebuked him roundly.

Well, shucks, they never did that again, of course. But I wonder, will history, ever record the time that a tugboat towed a towheaded kid, on a "surfboard," into Bonneville Locks?

Chapter 15

The Dubois Mill

Although the kid's tug was low enough to pass under the main, or lift span, of the Columbia River Bridge at Vancouver, Washington, without that span having to be lifted for them, still, that span was very close to the Washington shore. Many of their log rafts were destined for the Dubois Sawmill, a few thousand feet further down. The simplest method of landing the rafts at the mill would have been to pass through the span until they were clear, cut loose, and run to the tail of the last raft, hook on, stop the tow, and haul it into the waiting dolphin. But with a 60 hp tug and 1,000 feet of log rafts?

Well, when one is short on power, the captain has to think. And he was sufficiently short on power that he was certain he could not stop the rafts in that current. So just before the tail raft cleared the piers of the bridge, he hauled out for the middle of the river, the heavy rafts following in a circle to the left. Then he began a circle to the right, allowing for that limit of 45 degrees between the two rafts. Before they were even with the mill, he had the lead raft headed straight in, with the tail raft just swinging to follow.

For several minutes, although the rafts were rushing downriver with the current, the tug was free to maneuver, even upstream some, if it was needed. So they nosed into the waiting dolphin, caught a line around one of the piling, and just hung on, as the rafts swung in their 1,000-foot arc, finally landing against the mill boom.

The boys secured the rafts, dropped back to strip their rigging, and ran for the fuel dock, not realizing, or even really caring, I suppose, that anyone noticed.

But many years later, the foreman of the mill just upstream from the Dubois Mill, was, by some curious flow of events, talking to a family member. "Was that little tug," and he named it, "your family's tug?"

And when the response was affirmative, he said, "Well, let me tell you, every time they came in, if at all possible I stopped what I was doing and just watched. It was an incredibly daring, yet graceful, confident drama every time, as those two boys, and that little tug, swung those big rafts in, tied them up, stripped their rigging, and were on their way as if it were "just another day on the water."

At the time, the kid was innocently unaware that he was doing anything especially skillful, or dramatic, but it really was both. And a qualified observer had noticed.

Chapter 16
More Funny Things

A Nose Dive

Yes, there were funny things that happened. Oh, you might call them, "narrowly averted catastrophes," but, since they were averted, they were funny.

One time, the kid's tug and a larger, Company tug were running light back up the river below Bonneville. The main current ran 6 to 10 mph there, so the slow log tugs would run up the eddy on the Hamilton Island side as far as they could, dive into that current, and angle across to the slack water just before the lock's lower estuary.

The boys had the two tugs tied side by side so that they could visit one another. The small tug's engine was pulling, but all the men were in the wheelhouse, or galley, of the larger tug. The steering was being done from there; because her wheelhouse was on an upper deck, the visibility was better there. The small tug was on the starboard side, the side closest to the current.

As the skipper of the *Vulcan*, the larger tug, routinely swung out into the current, things happened rapidly. There probably was a 1 mph eddy, the tugs were making about 12, and the current coming down at about 8 or more. That added up to over 20 mph. Low, heavy, log tugs were not designed to sustain 20 mph through the water.

The little tug hit that fast water first, and for perhaps a hundred feet, the big tug was still in the eddy, driving the small one into that boiling flow. The small tug dove for the bottom; green water, two feet deep, poured over the forward deck and back toward the open, engine room door. Someone yelled and leaped for the wheelhouse of the small tug to cut the power, and the skipper of the *Vulcan* cut his; the two boats nearly stopped, as half the Columbia River poured off the deck of the little tug.

The slightly embarrassed but laughing crews cut the two tugs apart, and each ran for the locks on his own.

Oops, He Forgot

Another time, the kid was laying at the floating marine ways, in Portland harbor. This was before cutless rubber bearings had been developed for the propeller shafts. Someone had discovered that water lubricates metal rubbing against rubber even better than oil lubricates metal against metal, and certainly better than water lubricates the metal to metal wear. But those rubber bearings were not yet developed; so the shafts had, as in this case, two bronze sleeves shrunk onto the steel shaft, one at the prop, and one half way up, where the shaft exited the hull.

The sleeves turned inside a "babbitt" bearing. Babbitt is a soft, smooth, low-friction metal, with a relatively low melting point, but which also took most of the wear. The tug had needed a new propeller shaft, so new bearings were to be poured.

Since that was the only work being done, it was not necessary to dry-dock the tug. Instead, just the stern was lifted out, putting the bow down, but still safely above water. The stern bearing was poured, and the stern was lowered back into the water so that the young skipper would have a level bed on which to sleep. But, since the day was done, and there was more work to do on the boat the next day, the sling was left attached, with the hull just lightly resting in it. A three-quarter (fortunately) new tieline held the bow against the dock. All was secure for the night; or so all thought.

More Funny Things

Later, the kid slipped into that comfortable bed, about three and a half feet off the deck, and settled into peaceful sleep. He was secure; the lapping of water against the docks and hull, the hum of traffic in the harbor, were sweet music to a river man. He slept well—until 3:00 A.M.

Suddenly awake, he realized that his bunk was sloping forward. In the dim light, he put out his hand and touched water. The wheelhouse was full of water. He tried to open a rear window, but it stuck; he had only seconds, he knew, so he dove for a side sliding door, praying that it would not be jammed. But, since apparently it was starting to float in its slide, it slid open easily. The kid swam out around the sinking tug, and climbed up on the deck of the marine ways. The owners, who had an apartment on an upper floor, took him in and gave him a bed for the rest of the night.

The next morning, the men surveyed the situation. The tug was still hanging in that stern sling, and the bow, though a few feet under water, was hanging on that thread of a piece of three-quarter "manila" line.

A sling was drawn under the bow, the bow raised level with the river, and the tug was pumped out. The insurance company sent down a marine surveyor who assessed all the damage, even agreeing to pay for a new spring-filled mattress. He determined that a ship, or ships, passing in the night had thrown some swells over the bow and into the open, forward hatch, causing the sinking. The kid did not argue.

And now, 50 years later, the true story can be told.

Pouring the molten metal into that stern bearing was no problem, because there was room to get the ladle over the pouring hole. But that mid-bearing was a special problem. They had to bore a one-half-inch hole through the six-inch by twelve-inch beam that was the keel, and pour from the inside of the hull. The hole had been bored, but, because the hour was late, they had elected to pour the bearing the next morning. Sometime later, someone noted that the kid needed a level bed, so they lowered the stern into the water enough to level it. No one thought about that half-inch hole. It took until 3:00 A.M. the next morning, but it was enough to sink a tug right at her moorings, alongside a drydock.

I'm sorry that an insurance company had to pay a claim that they probably didn't owe. But still, I'll bet five dollars that if the claim adjustor is still living, he would laugh with the kid over this "narrowly averted catastrophe." After all, the kid could have drowned.

Nichols Towing Company tugs, *Louise N.* (left), and *Vulcan* (against barge), laying a telephone cable across the Columbia near Lyle, Washington, May 13, 1939. Captain Jack Frederick is standing on the foredeck of the *Vulcan*.

God's Eternal Why

Many years ago, when my first love was flying, a poem started, deep inside of me. One day, when the wings lifted me into the endless, blue sky, a song burst forth:

> Ah, such winged things we fly
> up in this wild and yonder
> everlasting sky.

The months and years passed; I came to Alaska, joined a flying club, and the northern skies amplified the song and added the words:

> Yes, poets write and angels sing,
> but could it ever be that Kings
> could ask for more than wings?

One day, perhaps eight or 10 years after the first words of the song became a part of my flying experience, the song asked for completion, and the last two verses came into being:

> For aeroplanes are not machines
> of soulless wood and steel and other things,
> but are themselves alive and free
> yet giving of that life to me.

> For who could ride upon the winds
> on wings in endless sky,
> and not believe those wings were part
> of God's eternal why.

April 1968
From the book *Islands of Experience*, by the same author.

Chapter 17

Sometimes the Bad Guys Won

Tom Ryan

Tom Ryan appeared to be a pompous, cigar-smoking business tycoon. At least that was the image he fairly successfully projected. But neither could he hide a good natured, likable, even loveable personality. He had bought the Underwood Log Dump from the kid's dad.

In the orbit of life in which we all seem to swing, the kid found himself, some years after "The Dubois Mill," rafting logs with his brother-in-law, Jack, again at Underwood. Tom was charging the loggers one dollar per thousand (1,000 board feet of potential lumber in the logs) and was paying Jack fifty cents per thousand to do the actual rafting. The kid, with just a bit of the skill at dickering and dealing he had inherited from his dad, had convinced Jack to pay him a percentage of his take, rather than hourly wages. So he definitely had an interest in the "scale" of each raft.

Although the rafts (pronounced by most rivermen, "ravs") were scaled by the licensed Columbia River Log Scaling and Grading Bureau, each month Tom would, in his pompous but loveable manner, bring a check down on the boom and present it to the boys. The backup document was just a handwritten slip of paper, showing the scale for each raft.

Most of the logs, by this time in logging history, were second-growth fir, and so were quite small, the average upper-river raft totaling around 110,000 to 120,000 board feet. There were still some big logs, however, and because they usually went to a different buyer, they were sorted out into their own, or "oversize" rafts. Their total scale would average around 220,000 board feet.

The calculating mind that the kid had inherited from his dad never stopped working. And, over the many years on the river he had, by sheer osmosis, developed a remarkable skill at accurately estimating the scale of each log, and even in an entire raft.

After some months, his mental computer sounded "alarm." The scale Tom was showing on his statement often seemed to be just a little short. He mentioned this to his brother-in-law employer. "You know, Jack, I could be just crying wolf, but then, why don't I drop in at the home of the resident scaler this evening. Their records are public records. I could get the official scale, and, if we're wrong, we can forget it. But if my suspicions are right, well . . ." So Jack gave his approval.

That evening the scaler welcomed the kid, and opened up his books. He too liked Tom Ryan, but fair is fair. So they went back through the last few months' records. And there it was. That scheming, loveable scoundrel had taken an even 5,000 board feet off each of the "peewee" rafts, and an even 10,000 to 20,000 board feet off each of the "oversize" rafts.

Actually, that was quite clever. By taking an even, or round number off, it left the last three digits of the scale intact, and so, not so noticeable. For example, a raft that scaled, honestly, at 118,426 board feet, would be shown on Tom's report as 113,426 board feet. So the kid made a list of all the discrepancies, and showed it to Jack the next day. Curiously, I don't think either of the boys was angry at the old scoundrel; and besides, the amount shorted on each raft, about $2.50 on an entire "peewee" raft, was so small that it was obvious Tom was doing it just for the sport of seeing if he could get away with it.

The next day, the boys were eating lunch down on one of the rafting gaps. Tom came moseying down. "Well, how are things going, my boy?" Tom asked Jack.

"Oh, fine, Tom, fine. We do have a bit of a problem with the scale though. Thought you might want to make some corrections." He presented Tom with the evidence.

Tom took the paper and started reading, then he read aloud, with almost convincing incredulity, "Five thousand, five thousand, five thousand, ten thousand, five thousand, five thousand, twenty thousand. Well, well, we'll take care of this right away, indeed; yes, right away."

And Jack answered, gently, but levelly, "Yes, Tom, I think that would be a good idea."

And Tom, unruffled, remarked a few more pleasantries, and walked casually back up the hill to his car.

Little Toot and the Big Boys

Whether truly deserved or not, Western Transportation skippers had a reputation, 50 years ago, for arrogance. The river was really theirs; the rest were interlopers, barely tolerated, like the driver one sometimes meets on a narrow lane, who barely moves over, expecting you to drive off into the mud to get around.

Still, the kid had little occasion to tangle with them, and their big barges and powerful tugs. But one dark and rainy night, he did tangle indeed.

Somewhere east of Vancouver, about at Fisher's Landing, the Corp of Engineers was dredging the river with a pipeline dredge. Their 15- to 20-inch pipeline, resting on pontoons, stretched nearly across the river. Occasionally, to let the river traffic flow, they would shut down the dredge and open the pipeline somewhere near its center.

On this night, the kid was upriver bound in that 38- foot, low, log tug, running light. The dredge had whistled that the line would be opened; but in the whelming darkness and against the bright lights on the dredge, it was unclear where the opening would be.

Sometimes the Bad Guys Won

But then, there it was, the pipeline lights were parting; the kid headed for the opening. But suddenly, from beyond the dazzling lights of the line and dredge, a powerful searchlight pierced the darkness, directed straight into the wheelhouse of the little tug. And it stayed there. A Western Transportation tug, twin screw, triple decked, and pushing a loaded barge, was charging for the middle of the opening, his searchlight clearly telling the small tug to stay clear.

It must be noted that shooting a searchlight into the wheelhouse of another vessel is not only very, very unlawful, it is also one of the biggest "no-no's" in the entire maritime industry. Only extreme arrogance would allow a man to do something far, far worse than even the violation of common courtesy. It was most fortunate for the captain of that big tug, that he had met just a kid on "Little Toot," that night. Had it happened just a few years later, he would have found himself being hauled before a maritime board of inquiry for that act.

Still, we all know how forgiving men are; men change; they grow. And so we know that, if the two captains were to meet today, the Western Captain would apologize, the "kid" would accept, and the two men would have many other stories to share. They would find themselves laughing together over the "good old days."

Chapter 18

A Burned Hand

The kid was really that, a kid, a boy tugboat captain, and he looked even younger than his 19 to 20 years. Still, and he looked even younger than his 19 to 20 years. Still, he had that intrepid, indefatigable dad who really believed in him. And he was the "signed-on" Master of a Documented Vessel. A documented vessel is any ship that is registered by a document, declaring its name as its identification, rather than by a number on the bow, as motorboats have. The Captain was then Master of a ship of the U.S. Merchant Marine. This gave certain privileges.

In those days, the Navy operated a hospital and clinic in Portland to which the crew-men on any documented vessel could go for free medical attention. All they needed was a claim form, signed by the master of the vessel.

Some years before the "Corbett Light" experience, the kid was running his tug on a contract job for building a string of channel-control jetties between Vancouver, Washington, and Multnomah Falls. In fact, they built the jetties featured in the chapter, "The Corbett Light."

But a boy becoming a man, needs some hard experiences, sometimes, to make the painful transition. He was not as sure of the authority he actually held, as he should have been. The rough pilebucks tended to run over him some.

A Burned Hand

One of the bad habits they had developed, done most often by a tall, powerful, and energetic pilebuck foreman, was to come running up, untie the boat, leap aboard, and yell, "Let's go." That was disrespectful in the least, and dangerous at the most.

So the kid's dad sent brother-in-law, Jack, down for a few days. He was older, and being a North Dakota farm boy, a little tougher. The tug was hanging off a barge on a single bow line. The foreman came running up, untied the boat, leaped aboard, and yelled his, "Let's go." Jack let the boat start drifting back in the slow current, and then yelled, "Grab a line, my engine's dead."

The panicked boss whirled around, leaped for the barge, now three or four feet away, narrowly averting a fall into the river. Just as he secured the line, Jack started the engine. When the somewhat shocked foreman came back aboard and stepped into the wheelhouse, obviously with furious words to say, Jack beat him to it with these quiet words of authority, "After this, don't untie the boat until we tell you to."

Relations were a bit strained for some time after that, but the kid had learned a rich lesson in his identity as a captain, however young he looked.

But back to youth and a burned hand. One day he was pushing a barge up the river along Government Island. He had not done a lot of that, so perhaps might be excused for forgetting about a line running from a stern cleat to the corner of the barge, and lying low to the deck near the engine room door. The kid himself almost always moved on a run.

Leaving that same, young foreman, now a friend, at the wheel, the kid dove for the engine room for some reason, tripped over that line, and literally dived toward the roaring engine. Instinctively, he put out his left hand to break his fall, and grabbed the nearly red-hot exhaust pipe. Struggling back to the wheelhouse, he showed the burned hand, now with a blister the size of his palm, to the foreman.

The foreman fashioned a bandage as best he could; they delivered their barge; the Company loaned a pickup truck, and the kid drove for that Navy hospital in Portland.

When he arrived, a doctor gave him emergency treatment, and then told the kid, "You must fill out this form, and have your ship's master sign it."

"Yes sir," the kid replied, and then filled out the form, and signed it, "Master."

The doctor looked at it, at the kid, shook his head in unbelief, and then grinned with belief, and even a bit of admiration, as he said to the attending nurse, "I thought this was the cabin boy who carne in, but this boy is the captain.

And for the several times after that that the kid came in for weekly re-dressing of that burn, that Navy doctor would say, in effect, "Well, here is the cabin boy who threw the captain overboard and took over."

Well, I can understand that. I too have noticed, as I've grown older, that doctors, and lawyers, and school teachers, yes, and tugboat captains, are getting younger and younger. Why, some of them are mere children.

Chapter 19
Fog Stories

A Curious Phenomenon

Since fog was rarely a problem on the mid-Columbia because of that nearly ever-present west wind, they carried no compass aboard the small tug. Still, a curious phenomenon occurred, about at Moffett Rock, a couple miles below Bonneville one night.

The kid and his dad were running light, upriver, and ran smack into a thick fog bank. The dad slowed the engine way down, peering hard to the right to catch glimpses of the stony cliff on the Oregon shore. Visibility ahead was zero.

They struggled on for some time, until the kid, looking down through the open side door, noticed that there seemed to be no fog close to the water. So he stepped out and knelt down on the damp deck. Two miles ahead, the brilliant lights of the Bonneville Powerhouse gleamed in the crystal air. There was a level "ceiling" of about six feet, all the way to the locks.

"Open 'er up, Dad," the kid hollered. "I can see all the way to Bonneville. I'll guide you from here." And they made the easy run to the locks above.

In the years that followed, the kid learned the almost incredible effectiveness of being on his knees in prayer; but that night was the only time he vicariously ran a tugboat through the fast water while kneeling on the deck of that small ship.

The Compass

I'm not sure that there is an official designation for lower Columbia, mid-Columbia, and upper Columbia, but the kid had always considered from the Willamette River to Astoria as the lower Columbia; Vancouver to The Dalles, the mid-Columbia; and The Dalles and east, the Upper Columbia. The mid-Columbia was divided into The mid, or Bonneville Lake, and the Lower mid, from Bonneville back to Vancouver.

I had said that fog was rarely a problem on the "midColumbia." But it would be more correct to say that it was almost never a problem on Bonneville Lake. But on the "lower mid?" Well, sometimes. Like the time he was serving his apprenticeship as deckhand for his brother-inlaw, Jack.

They had run light, in the daylight this time, as far east of Vancouver as the head of Government Island. The fog thickened, and so, with no compass, Jack laid the boat in against the island.

Brilliant visionaries are also capable sometimes of dreaming dumb dreams that is, if they work, they are brilliant; if they fail, they are dumb. Well, the kid's active mind remembered his high school physics. You can take a bar of soft iron, point it north and downward, in line with the earth's magnetic field, beat on one end with a hammer, and the molecules will re-align with the earth's magnetic field, and the bar will become a weak magnet.

Now there was really nothing else to do, laying there against Government Island, waiting on the fog; so Jack listened as the kid explained the physics involved.

"Well," Jack finally said, less than fully convinced, "We're going nowhere as we are; show me what you mean."

So the kid dug around in the engine room and found a one-half-inch steel bolt (hardly soft iron) and a hammer, pointed the bolt north and down, and started hammering. When he felt he had hammered enough, by what determination we'll never know,

Fog Stories

he tied a piece of thread to the balance point of the bolt, and suspended it to the overhead in the wheelhouse. The threaded end seemed to be pointing north.

"Well," the captain reasoned, "there's nothing really dangerous east of here, except a few jetties and a number of sandbars; let's try it." And they started up the river, keeping that threaded end of the bolt pointed slightly aft of abeam on the port side.

For half an hour, all seemed to be going well; they actually began to expect they would be finding the power line towers near the mouth of the Sandy River any moment.

When they ran aground, almost gently, on a long sloping sand bar, and the boat came to a stop, that bolt compass continued in a slow turn to the left. It was some time before the fog lifted enough so they could determine where they were. When it did, they were aground on the head of Sand Island, which lies between Government Island and Lady Island. They were less than half a mile from their starting point, a half-hour before. Only a pair of Guardian Angels knew where they had wandered in their six-mile circle.

Years later, the kid was running a tug for General Construction Company, on The Dalles Dam. A pilebuck foreman, generally pretty good, would occasionally have an idea that just couldn't work. He would force the men to try it every way possible. Finally giving up, he would be heard to mutter. "It was a good idea it should have worked."

As the fog continued to lift, Jack backed off the gentle sand, tore the bolt-compass down, and headed up the river "VFR." "Put that thing back in the tool box," he ordered.

Brilliant visions, or dumb dreams. Well, this one was not a brilliant vision, but only because it didn't work. It should have, it was a good idea.

Chapter 20
Other Funny Things

The Wrong Side

As in the chapter, "Funny Things," these two stories are also "narrowly averted catastrophes," or, as in the second, a narrowly averted tragedy. But, since they turned out OK, they were funny.

I believe it was on the Company tug, Ranger, and, for another change it seems, in broad daylight; the kid was again skirting that Sandy River Bar. He had a single log raft in tow and a passenger-friend for a deckhand. They were headed north, downriver, making to round the Washougal Dolphin. As said earlier, the river turned back west, right at the dolphin, so even a drifting raft would hardly have hit that dolphin, but would have swung wide, well on the Washington side. How could anyone make a mistake there?

About a mile above that turn, the deckhand reported that the skipper's lunch was ready. So simple instructions were given: "Swing the tug as close to that dolphin as you can, and then head west, a little to the right of that red buoy a mile down." The skipper ducked back to the galley and sat down; the tug rumbled on.

After years on the water, the trained or experienced ear hears any sound, or shift in sound, that tells volumes in information. Ten minutes or so into his meal, the kid heard the close echo of the tug's exhaust barking back from that dolphin. He glanced out the port window, but no dolphin. In a shock, he whirled around to see

Other Funny Things

the dolphin passing by, close on the starboard side of the tug. That meant the tug was passing on the port, or left side, of the dolphin; the raft, of course, swinging to the starboard, or right side. A bowstring was soon to come tight, and no arrow would fly.

Before he made the wheelhouse, the towline was already rubbing along the dolphin. And before he could speak, his innocently smiling helmsman asked, "Is that close enough, Cap?"

The kid grabbed the wheel and swung the tug in a tight circle to the left, nudged up to the raft to give it enough push to be sure to clear the dolphin, backed off, turned back to catch the towline tight, and continued down the river.

A Rude Awakening

It sure seems like a lot happened around that Sandy River bar. One very dark night, some years later, the kid was running the tug, *James Russell*, pushing a huge derrick barge. They had just cleared the Washougal Dolphin, upward bound. The river appears deceptively wide there, but the kid knew that just beneath the surface there was gravel on the right and sand on the left; the actual channel was probably less than one-third the total width.

The huge house on the derrick barge blocked forward vision for 80 or 90 degrees, but that left enough forward vision, at an angle, that, with the experience gained from many hours of peering into the river night, he was able to keep safely in the channel.

Actually, it was that blocked, directly forward vision that was a problem. I suppose that in today's penchant for pointing fingers, the kid could have been cited for failure to keep a proper watch forward. But heck, clearly they were the only ones on the river that dark night, and, though it was very dark, it was also very clear. So every 10 or 15 minutes the kid would climb down from the wheelhouse, scramble up through the machinery on the barge, and scan ahead for three or four miles, looking for the lights of any other traffic.

He had just come back from such a foray when cursing, shouting, and flashing of lights exploded at the lead edge of the barge. He shut the engine down; his deckhand ran forward, and soon shouted back, "We've run into a fisherman." The tow, making no more than 5 or so knots under power, was now nearly stopped. The kid also ran forward. A cursing, raving fisherman, his boat pressed broadside hard against the barge, was trying to fend himself off. The two boys helped him get clear, and the last they saw, or heard, a furious, frightened fisherman was drifting off into the night exclaiming his curses against heaven, earth, and, of course, all tugboatmen.

After the shock at what could have happened passed, the two boys laughed for days, as they reconstructed how that situation must have developed.

A driftnet fisherman, his lights off to save his battery, had gone to sleep, drifting down that quiet, empty river. What a shock it would have been to be shaken from sleep by the crash of what must have appeared to be a towering office building, slamming in from the side. His own sense of guilt for having his lights off, and for having gone to sleep, probably also contributed to his babbling confusion. He never reported the collision, and, of course, neither did the kid.

Life, even with its problems, was more fun 50 years ago.

Chapter 21
A Magnificent Vessel

The sternwheeler, *Jean*, was truly a magnificent vessel. As I recall her history, she was built somewhere around 1938 to 1940 by Western Transportation Company. Some old executives of the company wanted to have one last fling at building a sternwheeler before the diesel tugs, with their efficient, screw propellers, took over completely.

They robbed the engines from two retired sternwheelers and installed them in a new, steel hull, and named her *Jean*. That made four massive, double-action steam cylinders, turning two huge paddlewheels, side by side. From any distance away, she appeared to be a conventional, single-paddle sternwheeler. But, since the cranks on each paddlewheel were offset a bit to prevent them from ever being locked at dead-center, the paddles turned with an uneven gait, that is, there was a fast and a slow side to each cycle.

All sternwheelers had that characteristic "surge" to their wheelwash. But the *Jean*, with her twin paddles, was really unique. Rarely, if ever, were the two pairs of engines perfectly synchronized, so that surge oscillated back and forth between the two paddles. From as far away as one could see her from the stern, the powerful *Jean* could be easily recognized.

The kid knew her well and truly respected, even admired, her very much. Still, there was somewhat of a love-hate relationship toward that formidable river ship.

Those driving paddles, especially when she was pushing a light or partially loaded barge, threw up a stern swell perhaps three to five feet high. After a few miles, there was a string of those swells following for at least a mile or more.

I don't know how many times it happened, but from the lofty point of nearly 50 years later, it seemed like many times that he and his deckhand would be stripping rigging from their log rafts, in the quiet water at the Dubois Mill in Vancouver. And then would come the *Jean*, charging down the river with a half-loaded barge. The bow wave from the barge would shake them a few times, and the *Jean* would be gone. And then would come those rolling stern swells that rolled, and rolled, and rolled. How long? I don't know; but surely, it must have been an hour. Have you ever tried to knock the doglines off a log raft, with those logs leaping as much as two feet? For just a little while, she was not a magnificent vessel at all. Ah, but who could help but love the *Jean*?

Twenty some years later, the kid, a grown man now, was working in Anchorage, Alaska. A copy of *SEA Magazine* was in his hands. Suddenly commanding his attention was a photograph of an old friend, a Columbia River sternwheeler. And the caption read, "Aged *Jean* Finally Retires." And then the article went on to say, in essence, "After a long and illustrious career, a grand old lady has earned her rest at last."

So the kid wrote a "Letter to the Editor."

"Dear Sir," he wrote. "I take a bit of umbrage at your references to the sternwheeler, *Jean*, as aged, old, or tired. I was running tugs on the Columbia when she was built, and I still have 20 years to go before I can retire. If the *Jean* is aged, that must make me the Ancient Mariner."

The magazine, without a ripple, printed his letter in full, giving it the proper heading, "Prose of Ancient Mariner."

The sternwheeler *Jean*—she truly was a magnificent old girl.

Chapter 22
Flying Stories

The kid had an airplane. Ah, but what does that have to do with a boating story? Well, in this case, very much.

But before we tell that part, let me defer to the airplane buffs who are asking, "OK, what kind of an airplane?"

It was one of the finest, uncomplicated, light planes that the industry ever produced: A '46 T-Craft, with a 65 hp Continental engine that had been converted (easily) to a 75 hp by enlarging the intake valves, and turning the engine a few more rpms. But that little, two-place bird had other features that also made her a winner.

With so dependable an engine, turning a McCauley Metal prop, and with her resting on 1320 Edo Floats, she seemed to eagerly leap off the water as if a pair of angels was adding their joyful lift.

But a boating story? Well, the U.S. Coast Guard (U.S.C.G.) and the Federal Aviation Agency (FAA had a mutual problem: "When does an airplane become a boat, or a boat become an airplane?" So they agreed on a "rule": When it is in the air, it is an airplane, and subject to FAA rules; but when it touches the water, it is a boat, and subject to U.S.C.G. rules.

So now, begins that "boating" story: The kid had a minor medical problem, but one that required a weekly trip to Portland for a time. Would one drive, when he could fly? Of course not. And generally, that worked very well. But weather. Very, very rarely was there fog on the Mid-Columbia, or Bonneville Lake. That prevailing west wind blew that away. But from the dam on to Portland? What to do? The kid was not "rated" for Instrument Flight. But, he knew that river like the proverbial back of his hand. And, he never found a time where the fog had the visibility more than a mile below the VFR minimum of three miles, nor the ceiling much below the VFR minimum of 1,000 feet.

So he dropped down and kissed the water with those Edo floats, and became a boat, cruising along at a comfortable 50 to 60 mph, along a water pathway that was a clear highway to a riverman.

Traveling down past famed Multnomah Falls, angling on north to Phoca Rock and Cape Horn, then back southwest to Corbett, on west to Gary Island, then almost north, it seemed, to make a "Pilon Turn" around the Washougal Dolphin, west to a Nun buoy, left a little to pass under the power line (remember, he is now a boat) more or less west a couple miles, angling right a few degrees to pass between Government Island and Sand Island, and on a couple miles to a seaplane base on a slough on the backside of the old Jantzen Beach Amusement Park, he pulled up on a float, tied his plane (ah, should he have said "boat"?) down, and walked up to the highway and caught a bus to town. (For the purists, let me make a disclaimer here. These directions may, well, not be precise, but instead, they are presented as one might think about a drive down the Columbia River on a highway that, more or less, follows the river. The road goes from The Dalles to Portland, along the banks of the Columbia River. And the kid just "drove" his "boat" down the Columbia River. It was that uncomplicated.)

But, back to the story: "All in a day's work?" Oh, I think not, but rather, a vivid memory, treasured by the spirit of a kid on the river. And yes, he evidences a sense of "divided loyalties." He loved his boats, but then:

> Ah what winged things we fly,
> Up in this wild and yonder, everlasting sky.
>
> Yes, poets write, and angels sing;

But could it ever be, that Kings,
could ask for more, than wings?

The kid tugboat captain and a sea plane were good friends. The following is not a boating story. But, in these days of increasing intrusion by government into our lives, this story speaks well of a time when a federal agent was clearly human.

An Understanding Agent

The kid and his family had a lovely home, more especially lovely because of its truly magnificent view. It was built a couple hundred feet back from the edge of a 400-foot bluff, which rose a few thousand feet back from the bank of that magnificent Columbia River.

Flying home from work, where he was running a tugboat on the building of The Dalles Dam, it seemed reasonable to the kid to just fly by the front of the house, signaling for his wife to drive down a couple miles to the White Salmon River, where he secured his float plane, and pick him up. It seemed perfectly safe to him and to his family.

But one day, he received a very serious-appearing letter from the Aeronautical Agency that had a watchful eye on such things.

The letter read:

> "Dear Mr. Nichols, Your airplane, [And he gave the number] has been reported to be flying low over, and close to houses along, the bluff southeast of White Salmon. This report, if true, is in violation of Civil Air Regulations. We are taking no formal action at this time, but instead are appealing to your good judgment in restricting your flights to discrete distances.
>
> Signed, Sincerely,
> Federal Agent.

So the kid wrote back:

> "Dear Sir,
> Your astute observations are remarkably accurate. A young flying enthusiast and his family have a different

view of the same activity from that of a 'Public' who...
well, better stop there. Surely, there will be no problem in
making a few adjustments in my flying patterns.
And I do thank you for your understanding.

Respectfully,
Capt. Dean Nichols"

Of course, that was around 65 years ago, when people, and "the government," spoke the same language.

George

A sad day, a lovely day, but booze and boats belong not together. And, once in a while that combination grabs our attention, so that, I believe, we can spiritually stand back and see the glory of God's plan in stark contrast.

The kid had taken a job as deckhand on an LCM, Surplus Landing Craft, being used as a tender to a derrick barge, lifting steel to the daring men, high on that cold steel, so that they could fit the pieces together to form a strong and useful bridge across the mighty Columbia, near The Dalles, Oregon.

Now, he was a licensed captain, but the job paid well, and was much closer to home; and, the potential for advancement was there . . . although not at all in the way he expected.

He had sold those marvelous EDO floats and re-installed wheels on his beloved T-Craft, and was flying back and forth to The Dalles from his home, 25 miles west. A friend had a farmer friend just east of The Dalles City, who had a field of alfalfa where he said "Of course, he can land there. Won't hurt the alfalfa hardly at all."

So now begins our story: One morning the kid arrived a bit early and walked down to the construction base, which was on the Oregon side of the river, and just east of the city. George, the captain, was not yet there, so the kid climbed down into the engine room and started the two, 6–71 "Jimmies," about 165 hp diesel engines. He kicked them in gear to work them a bit and warm them up.

But the starboard engine, being cold and, the kid thought, reluctant to run on such a cold morning, died. So the kid climbed back down into the engine room, and re-started the engine. When he came back on deck, he saw George's coat lying on the deck, but no George.

As the crew started coming on board, each would ask, "Where's George?" And several would say, "He surely had been nipping the jug, for so early."

The crew all aboard, the superintendent asked the kid, "Can you run this thing?" And the kid answered him, "Of course." So the superintendent just said, "Take us to the rig" (the derrick barge).

As they were running out to the rig, the kid surmised to the crew, "He must have fallen between the boat and the dock, hit his head, and just did not come up. When I fly home this evening, I will circle the small island just downstream, and then search the Oregon shore all the way home. In the morning, I will search the Washington shore and circle the island and he should show up in a week or so." And so he did, a few hundred feet downstream, a week or so later.

And that evening, the crew all gone home (he thought), he spotted the body of that fine man, floating face down, just a few hundred feet downstream from the dock.

"Well, captain," the kid told himself. "You have a hard job to do." So he flew that 46 T-Craft back toward that alfalfa field. But as he flew over the landing, he noted that the small boat that he meant to use, the 24-foot wooden fishing boat, used mostly as a "safety boat," was not there. But looking across the river, he saw it tied to the derrick barge, and a "late repair crew" working there.

Breathing a sigh of relief, he flew over to the rig, buzzed them closely, and flew back to George, hoping they would follow. They did not, thinking that he was just showing off. Again he tried "buzzing" the crew. But no result.

So he circled inland a ways, shut down his engine, and glided down 40 or 50 feet above the crew, his side window open, and just shouted out, "I found George." Several waved their hands and ran for the boat.

The kid flew back to George's body and circled until the boat reached him; someone waved, and, with great relief, but surely with genuine grief, the kid flew home.

At one time, the kid could have named off 25 or more men that he knew, who had lost their lives to the waters.

The seas, and the rivers that feed them, are surely a gift to mankind. But as it is written: "They are terribly unforgiving of any carelessness, incapacity, or neglect."

The loss of George is part of the bittersweet drama of life itself. Let us return to the kid on the river.

> A river, even one of the major
> rivers of the world, is not the
> sea. Ah, but, is it not written,
> "The sea lives because the rivers
> ever reach its shores."

Land-Bound Lament

> The sea, the sea, the endless sea
> sends out its siren call for me.
> Yet oh that call, that haunting call
> cannot be heard by one and all,
> But only by the hearts attuned
> to sense the mysteries it holds,
> to feel its healing for my wound,
> to hear the challenge to the bold.
> A challenge that is not a dare,
> but rather invitation there
> to see your soul stand tall and free
> while held with awe of the endless sea.
>
> March 2, 1964
> From the book, *Islands of Experience*
> by the same author.

Chapter 23
Inventions

A Smooth Ride

The kid, with his mother's intelligence and his father's vision, was inventive; sometimes small, and sometimes big.

The old, heavy-duty, slow-turning Atlas, Fairbanks Morse, Washington, and Enterprise diesels were so out of balance, they would shake those resilient, wooden tugs like a diver on a springboard. Sometimes the bow stem, and the stern transom on a 60-foot tug would be moving up and down as much as six to 12 inches in perfect harmony with those massive engines. The yellow fir, Port Orford cedar, iron bark, oak, and other woods from which they were built, had a God-designed elasticity that never fatigued.

The kid's "high-speed" Atlas was, compared to the older engines, relatively smooth running. Still, at only 600 rpms, the vibration coming up through the hard wheelhouse deck, and into the hard legs of the helmsman's stool, could be very, very wearying after 40 or 50 hours of sitting and steering.

One day he was standing with four, stiff, discarded valve springs from an overhauled engine in his hand. Their inside diameter was only slightly less than the outside diameter of the stool legs. Perfect, he thought. So he whittled the bottom inch or so of each leg down just enough that the valve springs would slip over, jamming them in place. They extended a couple inches below the bottom of each leg. The engine and deck vibrations never reached the stool legs. Many thousand hours of smooth riding followed, with those discarded valve springs absorbing every bit of the vibrations, which the engine and that wooden hull could handle so easily, but for which a man's back and bottom were never designed.

An Illegal Lift

Once in a while there would be reason to get at the rudder or prop of that little tug, there in the White Salmon River. There was a dry dock in Portland, 65 miles away. And there was a steel-girdered, state highway bridge across the mouth of the White Salmon.

"You know, Dad," the kid said one day, "That towing winch is a five-ton Beebe. If we hung a pair of snatch blocks on a strap on that lower girder, and one on the sling under the stern, we could reeve a four-part line and lift the stern just out of the water. In theory, we could lift 20 tons." I don't know how many times they lifted the stern that way, and, of course, using a Washington state highway bridge for such an unauthorized load was very illegal. But, no one was hurt. You couldn't do a thing like that today, of course.

The Pike Pole

The kid's development of the aluminum pike pole was a very real breakthrough in the water-born arena of the logging industry.

The pike pole was *the* tool for handling floating logs. Around one and a half inches in diameter, and 12 to 16 feet long, they were made of turned wood. Some were of Douglas fir, lighter, but more easily broken. Some were of hardwood, strong, but miserably heavy. They all had a steel "pike" in the end, about four inches long, tapering to about one-quarter inch in diameter on the point. They could be thrown like a spear and driven into a log for pushing or pulling. With a slight twist, they could be easily pulled out. Without a pike pole, a "boomcat" was nearly helpless.

For years the only pike poles available were those commercially fabricated ones, or, as the kid and his coworkers preferred, a fir sapling, trimmed and sanded a bit so they could slide through the hands. Because they were naturally tapered, and the grain was

Inventions

not disturbed, they were both lighter and stronger than the commercial fir poles, and much lighter than the hardwood poles. But they were not the perfect answer, even so.

The kid had found a piece of aluminum tubing one day and wondered why that might not make a pike pole. So the next time he was in Portland with his dad, he walked down to a supply warehouse that stocked miles of aluminum tubing. He told the manager what he wanted to do, that is, to see if he could find just the right size and strength of tubing to make a practical pike pole. "You know," he told the manager, "If this works, as I believe it should, the commercial manufacturers could make lots of money building them for the industry."

The manager was either struck with the delightful audacity of this boy riverman, or he had vision himself, for he took the kid up on the second floor of a huge warehouse. There, stacked in rack after rack were miles of aluminum tubing of all sizes. "Take your pick," the manager said, "they are arranged in ascending sizes as you move down the row; they increase in wall thickness as you get closer to the floor." He stood back, watching and waiting.

The kid drew out a 12-foot piece, about one and one-half inches in diameter, and tested its strength against the floor. "Go ahead and break it, if you have to," the manager encouraged.

But the kid answered, "No, I don't need to do that; I can tell that that one is not strong enough." So he dropped down and tried a heavier one, then another.

Finally, he found the size, and strength he knew was right. "I really want a pike pole 14 feet long," the kid said. "These are only 12 feet."

"Well," the manager answered, "the next size down of the same wall thickness will exactly fit inside its next upper size."

So the kid bought the 12 foot, one and a half inch length, and a three-foot length of the smaller size, and carried them up the streets of Portland, Oregon, to his car. At home, he slipped the smaller tube about 18 inches inside the larger one and banged the outside of the overlap with a hammer hard enough to dent them both in a little. They couldn't move. Next, he drove a wooden plug in each end, bored a three-eighths-inch hole in the foot end, and screwed in a steel pike. It was light, and strong, and it never slivered. For years, as far as anyone knew, he was the only riverman with an aluminum pike pole. When the commercial companies finally started producing aluminum pike poles, (single piece, full length, of course) they were exactly of the size and wall thickness of the main portion of the one the kid built nearly 10 years before.

Joseph Peavey has his name forever engraved in the stone of history, because he modified the fixed hook on log rolling tools to a swinging hook, making them adjustable to almost any size log. The kid too, made history, but, sigh, it will doubtlessly never be recorded, except in these pages. But, he made history.

Bundled logs at the Nichols log boom, Hood River, Oregon about 1946. The system, widely used today, was invented and patented by Captains Dean and Luke Nichols. The men never made any money on the patent, but their work did mark a turning point in the history of log towing in the Pacific Northwest.

Chapter 24

The Big Invention

The kid's dad had an idea. He had lots of ideas, but over the years he mentioned this one every once in a while, and the kid kept thinking about it too.

The idea? Well, if one could pull a dozen or two logs into a bundle, and tie them there with cables, they would take a lot less room, and they would, or should, make much more seaworthy rafts.

One day, things were quiet at the Hood River log boom. "You know, Dad, why don't we experiment with that bundling idea. We could rig double lines on the drum of the donkey on our little A-frame scow, string them around a brail of logs, parbuckle them in, and see what happens."

The capable hands of the "old man" and his son soon had the rig ready and logs in place. It worked remarkably well; the logs tumbled together into a tight bundle, occupying about one-third the space. When they slacked the lines, the logs tumbled back to a flat brail. They pulled them in again, easily, and let them out, like l boys, playing with a new toy.

Well, a toy is fun, but they were in the towing business to make money. How to turn this simple but brilliant idea into money? An old friend, a one-legged lawyer, named Bob Garver, was called on. "Patent the idea," was his reasonable-sounding counsel.

About that time a shyster entrepreneur who busied around the river dropped in. He was given a demonstration of log bundling. The dollar signs gleamed like lights in his eyes. "No, don't bother to patent the idea," he counseled, "Let me get you contracts for bundling logs at the log booms up and down the river. Why, I can get you more business than you can handle, bundling logs just above the Oregon City locks alone. There is always a string of rafts waiting to lock through there."

But this was one time when the shrewd mind of the kid's dad listened to the wrong counselor. The entrepreneur, though apparently reasonably successful, was a crook; everybody knew that. The lawyer was an old, family friend. The patent process was started.

Special quick-release clamps for the cables were developed, and wire rope was spliced into the right lengths, all very specifically patented, and log bundling began at the Company log boom at Hood River, Oregon.

But, as said above, although in his search at the Patent Office the lawyer had found no similar patents, like the two men he went the logical, but opposite way he should have gone, and patented also the specifics. He should have patented the concept as broadly as possible, simply because the more specific the patent language is, the more easily it can be stepped around.

It is just possible that they could have patented the broad general idea of bundling logs. If they had, they would have had some control. Still, it would have been a never-ending war, fighting off the wolves. The lawyer friend, though not a patent lawyer, still did some excellent work; the blueprints, and writings are well done, but the rest of the industry just took the concept and ran.

The idea quickly evolved into simply building heavy enough A-frame hoists at each log dump to lift an entire truckload of logs at one time. A pair of steel bands were crimped around each load, which was then lifted off the truck, and swung out and lowered into the water. The bands were not re-useable, but they are less expensive than buying, maintaining, and handling all those wire rope slings and cast-iron clamps. This process lawfully bypassed the patent. But certainly, the concept of bundling logs that the fatherson developed revolutionized log towing and storage. And that was reward enough.

Some years later, the kid was parked with his girlfriend, down near Hood, across from and below Hood River. They watched with deep satisfaction, a tug successfully towing three rafts of bundled logs down a river that would have been far too rough for conventional, flat rafts.

He was not rich, nor did he really mind. The greater reward was, yet again, there in the river, knowing that he had had a hand in making history.

Chapter 25
Russell Towboat and Moorage Company

But They Have the Papers

Nearly 50 years ago, the kid was running, sometimes the *Altoona*, but generally, the *James Russell*, for Russell Towboat and Moorage Company. It must be remembered that this story is being told from the perspective of just kids, boy tugboat skippers. And to be true to history, we must record events as seen from those boys' eyes.

And as seen from the limited view of those boys' eyes Russell was, well, shall we kindly say, frugal. It seemed to the kid and a couple of the other young skippers that the Company would spend $50 to save $5, but the boys couldn't get them to spend $5 to save $50. Employees and employers seldom have a balanced view of things, I know.

These were war years, and good help was hard to find. Some of the deckhands they found seemed to have two legs, two arms, and something resembling a head but not much else. And of course, skippers were even harder to find. So Russell recruited some steamboat captains out of retirement.

Oh, these were grand old men, they really were. But they had left the trade with the deeply ingrained concept of a boat as a slow, plodding, never-in-a-hurry steam sternwheeler. It was really unfair to ask them to step aboard these high-speed diesel tugs, where 10 moves would be made while that old steamboat was just getting underway. They were good men, able men, but they were just thrust into an environment far too fast for them, without time to adapt. The time was not given.

The boys, on the other hand, had grown into the fast little tugs, and so handled them with the skill, confidence, and ease of driving their Model A roadster down the highway. Logic would follow that the more highly skilled employee would be paid the higher wage; at least that was the logic of the skilled, boy tugboat captains. But the Company had a different view: "But you don't understand, boys, they have the papers"(Master of Steam Vessel licenses).

Mere tugboats had not yet reached the status of being recognized as true vessels of the U.S. Merchant Marine, and so, of course, no license was required then to run a mere tugboat. The boys had no licenses; they just ran the tugs, captain in command, sometimes with thousands of tons and hundreds of thousands of dollars' worth of equipment held in the skilled touch of their hands.

What that "Master of Steam Vessel" had to do with the equation, the boys could not see; but that was what the boss said. The going captain's pay at the time was $235 a month, and "pilot's" pay was $215 a month. Actually, that was pretty good pay for the times, despite the fact that that was for six 12-hour days a week. And, the checks were always on time. But the hot, young skippers were paid pilot's pay, of $215 a month, even when totally in command, and the old steamboat captains were paid captain's pay of $235 a month.

Young Lew Russell, Jr., a contemporary of the kid at the time, is now chairman of the board of Russell Towboat. A couple years ago, the kid and Lew sat at dinner together, equal members of the Loyal Order of River and Wharf Rats. The kid's title is Chief Waiting Rat, because he waited six years for the opportunity to come down from Alaska and join.

Every second year, this lowly group, this most informal, ad hoc group of old River and Wharf Rats (including such present-day captains of industry as Lew Russell, Jr.; "Slim" Leppaluoto; George Shaver; and old-time marine lawyer Chief Legal Rat Tom White) meets at the University Club in Portland to share those marvelous reminiscences of "the good old days" on the water. But they meet also to honor, with the sounding of a baleful air horn, those old "Rats" who have crossed the bar since the last meeting.

But sitting there in the glow of that grand camaraderie, the kid didn't have the heart to press Lew on that unfair discrepancy of so many years ago. Perhaps, when he reads this now, in the wisdom of his years, he will smile and say, "No, that wasn't quite right, was it?" And the kid will grin and fully accept the indirect apology.

A Flying Coffee Pot

We've heard of flying horses, and flying nuns, and flying houses, but this is the story of a flying coffee pot—a full, one and a half gallon, hot coffee pot.

The kid and one of the old steamboat captains were running the *James Russell* at Moffett Rock, a couple miles below Bonneville. A contractor had drilled and blasted, and was now digging the broken rock out to make the channel safer at that narrow point. The kid and the old captain, let's call him Captain Olson, were operating the tug on opposite, 12-hour shifts.

But for some reason, both men were aboard one day as the *James* had been hired to help push a heavy tow on past the dredge, and up to the locks in that fast water. And, curiously, both men were in the galley on the main deck, just below the wheelhouse, a hot, one and a half gallon, full coffee pot on the big, oil range. Probably, Lew Russell, Jr., himself was running the tug.

As I've said, these were war years, so the U.S. Coast Guard was charged to inspect every tow, up or down the river, for possible explosives that saboteurs might use to blow up the locks. The small, but powerful Coast Guard boat had just been alongside for his inspection. The whole tow was making maybe 8 knots through the water, but with a 6 knot current, they appeared pretty slow at only 2 knots upstream.

As the Coast Guard boat pulled away, he courteously kept his engine slow for several minutes, and then poured on the power That powerful, little ship dug a great big hole in the water, and, because of the current, that hole never followed him upstream at all, but just rolled sideways to the *James*.

All of a sudden, the *James* rolled 15 to 20 degrees to the starboard. Both men caught their balance OK, but that coffee pot came off that stove, three or four feet away, flying right in front of the kid. He was probably gesturing at the time, because the handle of that coffee pot was suddenly in his hand. The *James* made only that one roll, settled herself back on even keel again, and the kid set that full, boiling coffee pot back on the stove. Not a drop was spilled. It really was just a case of being in the right place at the right time, or more narrowly, in the right spot at the right second; but it did appear to be a mighty spectacular "fly ball" catch. Captain Olson was so impressed I'm sure he told that story to his grandchildren until the day he died. Someday, in Heaven, he and the kid will laugh again about that incredible catch of a flying coffee pot.

The Miracle of Wood

The broken rock from the reef was being lifted out by a bucket dredge and dropped into the hoppers of a dump scow. The kid was just making up to that scow with the *James* when one of the old steamboat captains in, I believe, the wooden tug *Altoona* came swinging into the side of the scow. He didn't realize that, though relative to the scow, he was hardly moving, relative to the current he was racing along at 6 or 7 knots. He made his correction for landing way too late and slammed sideways into the massive corner of the scow with an incredible crash.

The kid, up in the second deck wheelhouse of the *James*, was looking right at the spot of collision. The gunnel of that tug was crushed in 16 to 18 inches. He saw it happen. No, not three or four inches, 16 to 18 inches. The kid expected the tug to be sinking in minutes.

But that old man must have reached his own golden years with the aid of his own Guardian Angel. The tug didn't sink. Sometime later they had opportunity to inspect the damage. They could find none.

Yes, I know, the old growth woods from which those beautiful old vessels were built did indeed have a remarkable, God-designed resiliency in them, but the kid saw that gunnel, deck, ribs, and engine house, slam in *16* to *18* inches and spring back out again.

But a thorough inspection showed no splinters, no cracks, no marks at all on that tug. A Guardian Angel had indeed done his work.

The Extra Mile

"And whosoever shall ask thee to go a mile, go with him two." Matt. 5:41.

The old captain was scared. But he was also honest. The digging of that rock was so slow, there was only one or two barge loads a day. "Kid," he confessed, "I've taken a barge load down to the dump site in the daylight, but

I'm not sure I can do it in the dark; and the way it is going, there will be a full barge about midnight. Could you come back and take her down for me?"

Well, what are you going to do, remind him of the difference in pay scale? Remind him of "those papers"? Of course not. So the kid went home for supper, asked his wife to fix an extra lunch, and went back, to sleep on the tug until the dredge whistled for a barge move. Russell probably never knew, and the kid didn't really care. That fine old man had paid his dues years before. Instinctively, the kid knew that he was simply investing in his own future.

A Wild Ride

Those old, wooden dump scows were miserable things to push. We've talked about log rafts "digging in their heels." Well, those dump scows were nearly as bad. The hoppers were built right down through the barge, with heavy, steel doors on the bottom to hold in the material. Winch lines ran to the doors to hold them shut. When the tug reached the dump site, the deckhand would go forward with. A dog axe or hammer, and knock loose the "dogs" on the winches. It was a terrible job. When the load of muddy rock fell to the bottom of the river, it left, for a moment, a huge hole in the water. But a second or two later, the laws of physics prevailed and muddy water rushed back in, and, of course, all over everything, especially that deckhand. And there were about three or four hoppers on each barge.

But this story is not really about dump scows in themselves, except that they were so hard to push. In fact the James Russell, with her 200 or so horsepower engine, could just barely push an empty barge back up the fast water to the dredge. So now, the drama begins.

Fortunately, it was broad daylight. Knowing that the tug could not begin to push that loaded barge against that racing current, the men would secure one corner stanchion of the barge to the dredge with wraps of heavy manila rope. Then while the tug was making up to the scow, they would ease off and cut loose the steel, breast line, and the heavy, steel spring line, leaving the whole thing hanging on the multiple strands of the manila rope. When the tug was ready, a dredge deckhand would unwrap the manila rope and stand clear; the line would fly off like a whip, and the tug and tow would rush away, backwards down the river. Normally, it worked quite well. Normally.

But this day, either the deckhand failed to hold that rope, or it just broke. The kid had not fully made up to the scow; that is, his bowline was secured, but his side lines, from the stern of his tug to the corners of the barge, were not yet on. The dredge crew had cut loose the upper breast line and were easing off on the spring line, putting the entire load on that manila rope. For whatever reason, it didn't hold, the scow dropped against that spring line, and the upstream end of the scow swung left, and into the current, broadside to that rushing flow.

Had the kid's starboard sideline been secured, the turning barge would have hauled his tug crossways, up into the current, probably rolling her over. But with that line not yet on, for 90 degrees of the scow's turn, at least, the tug could "weathervane" with the current.

Before the scow reached past that critical 90 degrees, that three-quarter to seven-eighths, steel spring line to the dredge broke with a bowstring crack heard even above the roar of the rig or the rush of the river. Tug and scow went cartwheeling down that racing waterway, but at least they were free. In a mile or so they were properly made up to the scow and proceeded to the dump site.

All in a day's work? No, hardly. But did anyone see that big, Guardian Angel cut them free from the spring line?

Someone once asked, "How do you determine who is a successful man?" And the wise answer, "If he has survived to the age of 65, you have to call him successful."

And I would add, "If he is still the chairman of the board of a continuing towboat Company, as Lew Russell, Jr. is, then he is doubly successful."

This chapter is, therefore, dedicated with true respect and affection to Captain Lewis Scott Russell, Jr., and Russell Towboat and Moorage Company.

[Captain Russell informs me that he has since sold the Russell Companies. But the above credits still stand.]

Chapter 26
Portland Tug and Barge

Captain Desmond E. Stanenko

I think he was probably Greek, tall, dark, handsome. But he was also quite aware of those good looks, for he was often heard to say, "If only I had seven million dollars instead of all these good looks . . ." The statement was never finished. He knew the hard reality of life; that trade was not likely to take place.

    Captain Stanenko was a skilled skipper, and one of the chief captains for Portland Tug and Barge, headquartered just above the St. Johns Bridge, on the southwest side of the Willamette River in Portland harbor. When the kid first met him, the kid had been hired to replace, for a few weeks, the pilot on the *Watco*, a 95-foot wooden tug with a 320 hp, Fairbanks Morse diesel engine. That beautiful engine had developed a "thump" in one of those massive connecting rods. So Captain Stanenko, a skilled diesel mechanic also, had been pressed into service "scraping in" a newly babbitted bearing. It was slow work.

    A special, thin dye, called "bluing," was painted on the bearing, which was then laboriously bolted into place; the engine was turned over a few turns, the bearing was removed, and from the re-distribution of the dye, he could tell where to carefully scrape on that soft babbitt to more perfectly fit it to the crankshaft. Frequent coffee breaks were, of course, "very necessary" for such "exacting" work. Captain Stanenko would sit, and wait, and visit, and wait. Invariably someone would say, " Your coffee's getting cold, Cap."

And always his quick retort, "I hope so, I hate lukewarm coffee." It made for extended coffee breaks. That, plus another characteristic we'll speak of later, most surely did not win the goodwill of the very able, but high-strung dispatcher, Mac LaRouche. Mac did have his point. But it was Stanenko's lightning, often devastating retorts that also won for him the fury of the girls in the office.

A master at the psychological "game" of "Courtroom," he would quietly step into the office and strike up a conversation with the girls. At first, it was no problem, but he would skillfully lead the girls into making some firm statement, any statement, and then he would cut the very foundation from under that statement with just a few quiet, but stabbing words. The girls would become so furious that, after he was gone, they would vow together, "The next time he comes in none of us will speak to him."

But that didn't work. Captain Stanenko would step into that silent office with icicles everywhere. He would just smile that handsome, winning smile, lean against the counter, and wait. Then he would make some totally unthreatening remark like, " Nice day." After a while, one of the girls would take the bait. A light, gentle conversation would develop; others, disarmed, would join in. I don't know how long it took, but perhaps in less than half an hour, one or two of the girls, without realizing how it happened, would be led into making their "firm statements," others would agree; they had him. And then would come the laser beams from that slicing tongue. The psychological demolition was complete; fury ruled, for a while, over the office work of Portland Tug and Barge. Mac LaRouche really had reason to hate Captain Desmond E. Stanenko, however much the Company needed his piloting skills. Curiously, he never played that game of "Courtroom" with the kid, so the two became good friends. But the office girls? And Mac LaRouche?

Portland Tug and Barge

Direct Reversibles

For a while, after the engine was repaired, the kid operated that big tug, with a different captain, as pilot, skipper in command on the opposite watch from the captain. It was really fun, and a whole new experience. The kid had always run tugs with reverse gears, transmissions, if you will, so they were easily shifted back and forth between forward and reverse. But the big, 320 hp Fairbanks Morse was direct reversible; that is, to effect reverse, the engine was shut down completely, and then restarted in the opposite direction from the limited supply of compressed air in the tanks. Although that gave marvelous reversing power, it was a slow, cumbersome process, and, because each start used a Lot of air, it was most limiting when juggling around in close quarters. Although there was a compressor cylinder on the rear of the engine, it took half an hour, or maybe an hour, to replenish the supply of compressed air. The skipper learned to plan each move, well ahead, and with great care. The kid learned.

But later, the kid was transferred, as pilot, to the *Superior*, about a 50- or 60-foot, wooden tug; Captain Desmond E. Stanenko in command. I believe the tug had about a 200 hp Superior diesel, but it too was direct reversible, and, because it was a much lighter tug, mistakes in judging the timing on that direct reversing were much more evident. The kid learned again.

One night, on the dogwatch, midnight to 6:00 A.M. (the pilot always stood the dogwatch), Captain Stanenko was sound asleep in his bunk. The kid had to move a small raft of peeler blocks, very short, but large chunks of logs. They were almost impossible to walk on. His deckhand was having a terrible time. The kid, trying to make things easier for that deckhand, forgot about watching that telltale, air pressure gauge. On one start, the engine barely started. Fortunately, he was pushing in against the raft. He had no choice, he just let that tug push against that raft for that half-hour or so, building up his air. The captain slept blissfully on. The deckhand suffered in the cold dark. The kid never told anyone of a hard lesson learned that night.

Captain Stanenko Again

According to "the rules," when there was less than a full crew on a double-crewed boat, the three remaining men had to be paid for any hours the tug was in operation; whereas, if there was a full crew, each skipper and deckhand was paid for 12 hours only each day. Hmm, it paid more to be short on crew; there was plenty of time for sleeping on the long, rock-barge hauls the *Superior* was making. So Captain Stanenko's remarkable cleverness went to work.

First, if Mac LaRouche was able to find some unsuspecting boy for the second deckhand, the captain immediately assigned him to the bunk, up over the big, iron, oil range in the combination foc'sle/galley. It was miserably hot. Then that slicing tongue of the captain would complete the torture, none of which was visible on the body, of course. No second deckhand lasted more than a few days. The kid never complained; after all, he wasn't the captain, and besides, 12 hours straight time, plus 12 hours overtime each day was pretty good pay. And anyway, the Company was making money, wasn't it?

Portland Tug and Barge had a real company man in dispatcher Mac LaRouche, but his understandable hatred for Captain Desmond E. Stanenko mush have brought great suffering into an innocent man's life.

An Unintended Dump Scow

Most of the barges were still made of wood; strong wood, fine-grained wood, but wood. Knapton, and perhaps others, still had some wooden oil barges. Some of that oil-saturated wood must still be around today.

The rock barges that the *Superior* was pushing up from Mt. Coffin, on the lower Columbia, were flat decked, wooden barges; they were not " dump scows." At least, they were not meant to be. One clear night, probably around 11:00 P.M. (because Captain Stanenko was on watch, with the kid asleep in his bunk), they were pushing two rock barges in tandem up the Willamette below the upper end of Multnomah Channel, each barge heavily loaded with three or four hundred tons of rock.

The Willamette makes a slow turn to the north about at Multnomah Channel. Far ahead, the captain saw a spoonbilled gravel barge coming down, the small tug hidden behind the huge piles of gravel.

Those spoonbilled barges were also wood, but they were massively built, and that curved bow added strength. The tugboatmen loved them because they pushed so easily.

Captain Stanenko was properly holding to the right of the channel, the southwest side. But as that gravel barge came on around that slow curve, it was evident that he was holding to his left, also the southwest side. So the *Superior* held even closer to that shore. As it turned out, it was such a small tug pushing that gravel barge, he had made up to the port, stern corner of his tow, because he could not see over that gravel. Apparently, hoping to stay clear of ships or other center channel traffic, he was holding closer and closer to his own left. Why he was not made up to his starboard corner, no one knows.

By the time he saw the *Superior*'s barges, and the *Superior* was unable to move further right, it was too late to avoid a collision. That massively built, spoonshaped bow of that gravel barge took the port, bow corner out of the lead rock barge. When he saw that they were going to hit, Captain Stanenko hollered at the kid, who leaped out of his bunk, hauled on his trousers, and climbed the ladder to the wheelhouse. But in those few moments, the lead barge had filled with water, tipped to the left, dumped her entire load, and was just settling back on an even keel. That old, wooden barge was not meant to be a dump scow, but it was one that night.

A Crystal-Clear Night

It is said that bad things run in threes, but for Portland Tug and Barge that winter, these two would have been enough.

A short time after that rock-barge incident, a pair of small, Company tugs were both dispatched to return home from Vancouver. They had a piledriver to take with them,
so they decided they might as well both push it home. They each made up to a corner of the barge. Besides, they could see ahead better that way.

It was so clear out that one of the men remarked, "Look how clear it is; why you can see that oil barge coming out of the Willamette down there." It was three or four miles away, but they could clearly see the outlines of the tow.

The two tugs started down the Columbia for the Willamette; the oil barge came up the Columbia. When they collided, the smooth rakes of that steel, oil barge ran right over that wooden piledriver, sending it to the bottom. I don't think anyone was hurt, and I'm sure the piledriver was salvaged. But two "bad things" were not enough for Portland Tug and Barge, that winter. There was to be one more.

Tragedy at Mt. Coffin

"If you have faith as a grain of mustard seed, you shall say unto this mountain, move from here to yonder place, and it shall move." Matt. 17:20.

I don't know that the men who began to quarry Mt. Coffin had that scripture in mind, but their faith in the quality of the rock in that mountain paid them well over the relatively few years that it took to remove that mountain. Good rock for riprap was, surprisingly, hard to find. The best deteriorated, or eroded slowly from the elements, and, was heavy. The rock in Mt. Coffin had both qualities. Curiously, granite, the stone most people associate with strength and permanence, is much too light for good riprap. Heavy waves will roll it away. But Mt. Coffin rock stayed, so it was barged for many miles up and down the river until, one day, Mt. Coffin was no more.

And I don't know why Mt. Coffin was named that, unless that, before man began to blast and quarry the hard, heavy rock of the mountain, it looked like a coffin.

But on one of their many trips down for rock barges, real tragedy struck. This is a sad story; I don't want to tell it, yet feel I must.

It was 2:00 or 3:00 in the afternoon of a cold, cold, dark, winter day. The temperature was below freezing; ice was forming here and there on the piling. The kid and his deckhand, George, were on watch and starting to make up to a loaded rock barge. In due respect for his family, George should not have been on the river; he was just not as alert as that dangerous work called for. And, having previously worked at a local shipyard, he had on a pair of heavy "shipyard" boots, excellent for protecting one's feet from sharp steel, but not at all the foot gear to be worn where any moment one might have to swim for his life.

George was standing down on the low deck of the barge, reaching for the port side line. The kid, meaning to help, flipped the line over to him. Somehow, George's hand got painfully pinched. As he jerked it back to nurse his wound, he took an unconscious step, and stepped off the barge into that frigid water. He just gasped, terrified gasps, and beat the water with his hands and arms stretched straight out to each side.

The kid, having fallen into that water hundreds, maybe thousands of times himself, was not particularly alarmed. He just climbed down on the rubber fenders on the bow, stuck his foot right in George's face and called, "Here, George, grab my foot." But the glazed eyes of panic did not see. So the kid scrambled to the deck and yelled, "Man overboard." Captain Stanenko, who had just gotten up to go to the head, buttoned his pants and ran to the foredeck.

"My God, kid, he can't swim!" he shouted.

This whole thing happened in far less time than it takes to write about it. The kid answered, "Well, throw the lifering in. I'll go after him," and jumped into that icy water. The crew on deck thought that the kid, himself, was in trouble, because he could not speak, but the shock of that cold water would not let him. Just before he reached George, who had drifted 10 or 15 feet away, George gave up and slowly sank below the surface, those heavy boots pulling him down. The kid tried to reach him with his own feet, but he was a second or two too late.

The Coast Guard was notified to come and do their grisly work of dragging for George's body, and the tug crew took their barge to Portland, arriving there late the next afternoon. As often happens, the full shock of seeing death right before one's eyes, and of coming so close, yet so far from saving one from that death—the full shock does not strike until sometime later. That next evening, the kid most gratefully accepted an invitation to the home of a friend of the captain's. He just couldn't be alone for a while.

And for Portland Tug and Barge, three "bad things" were indeed enough for one cold winter.

Overboard

We must end the saga of Portland Tug and Barge on an up note. They made their rescues, too. Another Company's tug was running light, up the Columbia a mile or two above Vancouver. A Portland Tug and Barge tug was running north there from behind Tomahawk Island. The helmsman was looking ahead, straight at the other tug, a half-mile or so away. The wheelhouse side door opened, a deckhand stepped out, closed the door and turned to descend the ladder to the lower deck. He apparently tripped, or slipped, missed his handhold, and dove over the side. The Captain innocently continued on up the river at full speed. The P. T. & B. tug continued straight ahead and picked up the swimming deckhand. It was some time later before an apologetic captain took his shivering and dripping deckhand back aboard and handed the deckhand that hot cup of coffee he had sent him to the galley to fetch. Most river stories turned out well. But clearly, again, a Guardian Angel was close by a startled young man that day.

Chapter 27
The Army

A War On

There was a real war on, in Europe, in the South Pacific, and in the kid's heart. His dad really did need him on the tugs, he knew that, and his wife and three beautiful children really did need him at home. So he listened to his dad's urging, and accepted deferment based on those three children, and a high-priority job as tugboat skipper.

But every month or so, one of his old school chums, and even his younger brother, would "go off to the war." It wasn't really fair, he knew; his own life was just as valuable for sacrifice as theirs. So he finally gave in to the call in his heart, and signed a "Voluntary Induction." In a short time he was called into the service, and sent to Fort Lewis, Washington.

There they were run through the ceremony, and that's all it was, of course, a ceremony of choosing their branch of service. For just a little while, the inductees were free to talk with any of the three recruiters there, Army, Navy, and Marines. Not knowing at the time that the Army actually has more boats than the Navy, and, that God has His own plans, no matter how firmly we make our own, he chose the Navy recruiter, and presented his case. "I'm a boat man, a skilled tugboat man; I belong on boats; I can best serve my country on boats; I want to join the Navy."

The recruiter was practiced at sympathetic denial. The quota for that day was, Army. "I surely understand, kid, but the Army has needs too. I can't take you; go to the Army man." And so, the "Captain of a Documented Vessel," became a private in the Army, a slugging doughboy, and was sent to Camp Roberts, California, for four months of basic training.

But he didn't give up. He prayed, and he went to see chaplains, and pleaded his case, "I am a boat man." He received sympathy, but no transfer. And all the while he was developing his skills as a tough, ground fighter. Chosen as a squad leader, he won medals for expert rifleman, and tactics, and map reading, and other skills, and even taught classes in rifle and machinegun disassembly and re-assembly. But the sea water in his blood never evaporated, but continued to resonance with the call of the sea.

San Francisco

With graduation from Basic Training, and a three-weeks' leave slip in his hand, he was picked up by his wife and his dad for the 500-mile drive home. They would pass through San Francisco. The kid had learned the name and office address of the full colonel who was in charge of the Army tugs on San Francisco Bay. The kid determined, "This man will understand." A full colonel? Well, the kid was really a civilian, a riverman at heart; rank did not disturb him. So they stopped in San Francisco.

The sergeant at the reception desk turned slightly pale and almost gasped, "You want to see the colonel?"

"Yes," the kid insisted, and was finally ushered in.

But the colonel was a harried manager of a fleet of tugs; everybody, has problems; and besides, this Army buck private was not going through channels. "Sorry, kid, I cannot (or will not) do anything for you."

The kid's mother's prayers were not working, and his dad's, "God helps those who help themselves," counsel was not working either.

The Army

Home Leave

When they reached home in White Salmon, Washington, the kid's younger brother was there on leave from the Coast Guard, which always is, during wartime, a part of the Navy. The boys renewed their filial bonds, and had great fun, wearing each other's uniforms and disturbing the hometown populace, who "knew" that the kid was supposed to be in the Army, and his brother in the Navy.

But time, always on the wing, flew away. They each put on their assigned uniforms again; the brother was sent to the Pacific Theater as engineer on a patrol craft, a miniature destroyer, P.C. 590. And the kid was shipped to Tackloban, on Leyte Island, in the Philippines, as just another of a pool of several thousand doughboys, waiting to be assigned to a unit.

Peace

The kid found the local chaplain. "Sir, there are over 7,000 islands in the Philippines; the Army has boats; I'm a boat man; see my credentials."

The chaplain was sympathetic, probably even prayed with the kid, but the kid went back to his camp, still an infantry rifleman.

During the short weeks in that depot, the kid developed friends, good friends. One day, a stark realization came to him. "These are good men; if they can fight in the mud, live, and die for one another here, in these jungles, then I *can* too." And a peace came over him, a palpable peace that had to be from God. His surrender was complete; he was content, but most of all, at peace. He would return to the waters another day.

The 532nd

Within just a few days of that surrender, 200 men were told to pack their duffel bags, issued light, .30 caliber rifles, and loaded onto trucks. They were being assigned to a unit. The 200 names had to have been just a block, taken off a roster, with one thing only in common: They were infantry riflemen. To the kid's knowledge, he was the only one with boating experience. But they had been assigned to the Boat Battalion, 532nd Engineers, Boat and Shore Regiment, Second Engineers Special Brigade.

The very next morning, the boys received their first pleasant shock. They had been used to standing in a long chow line, at an Army Depot, holding out their mess gear for the unimaginative Army chow to be slammed into their plates. This morning heaven smiled. The cook, serving the man about three men up the line, called down. "How do you want your eggs?"

"How do I what? You mean I have a choice?"

"Yeah, how do you want your eggs?"

The kid stammered something like, "Over easy," and stepped up in the line as it moved. If heaven was a chow line on a South Pacific island, then this was heaven.

In another few days, the men were loaded aboard an LCI (Landing Craft Infantry) and sent around to Ilo Ilo, on Panay Island. Of course, their censored letters home merely read, "Somewhere in the Visayas." But they spent a few, short months staging there for the major, diversionary attack on Japan. Had those powerful weapons not been dropped on Hiroshima and Nagasaki, thus ending the war, the 532nd would have been a spearhead, sent in in an attack from the northwest, intended to draw most of the defending Japanese Army down upon them, while the main attack slammed in from below. It would have been a bloody battle. However the anti-nuclear apologists may try to argue, those two nuclear bombs, while killing a few hundred thousand Japanese, ended a costly, costly war, and saved well over one and a half million lives, half at least, America's finest.

The Yellow Sea

In just a few weeks after the Japanese surrender, the 532nd was loaded aboard an LSD (Landing Ship Dock) and hauled up the Yellow Sea to Inchon, Korea. There, the kid was assigned as captain (the Army called it coxswain) of a 37-foot, 225 hp, landing craft.

The Army

The "well deck" was covered with a framed and painted canvas, making the quarters for coxswain, deckhand, and engineer, each with his own, warm cot. Generally they ate aboard; food was abundantly available to scrounge from the steady flow of supply boats. They were on duty as water taxis for 24 hours, and then free for 24 hours. They had a private yacht, an unpolished one, perhaps, but a private yacht, all expenses paid; and they burned as much, or more fuel on their days off than on their duty days.

There was around a 30-foot tide on the sea there. In fact, it was obvious, once there, why it was so named. The tides rushed in ebb and flood with such force, they kept the yellow mud constantly stirred up. It was very literally, a yellow sea.

Family Bonds

But with those 30-foot tides, the big ships had to anchor out in the roadstead, seven to 10 miles out the channel from the protected inner harbor. The water taxis hauled Army, Marine, Navy, and Merchant Marine men back and forth. On the long run out, the kid seldom failed to exact an unofficial fee of some fresh bread, fruit, or meat from one of the always well stocked ships.

But shortly after establishing their base there, the kid was on a run out to that outer harbor. Cruising slowly up, among the anchored ships, was P. C. 589. For just a few moments, the possible nearness of family almost stopped the heart of a lonely sailor, somewhere on the backwaters of the Yellow Sea. One digit off from his brother's P.C. 590; so close, but it was just a number. He did not know that P.C. 590 had lost a battle with a typhoon about that time, and, though his brother survived, he was, for some time during that storm, battened down in the engine room of that grounded ship, keeping those engines and pumps going, and all the while not knowing if they would ever breathe free air again.

The bonds of family; they never break, nor should they.

Two Captains Meet

In a very short time, the kid's boat-handling skills, developed since childhood, conquered that simple, Army boat. He and his craft became one. They danced together over that yellow sea. One day they were dispatched out to the roadstead to pick 15 or so men off a merchant ship. The wind, blowing against the rushing tide, was kicking up a mean, three- or four-foot chop. The ladder (actually a stairway) down the side of that ship ended in a raw, steel landing, a few feet off the water. That sharp steel was like angry teeth, waiting to chew into the sides of that plywood boat.

The forward two-thirds of that landing craft, flat bottomed and lying shallow in the water, yet a box above water, was almost a sail, moved by every puff of wind. At very low speeds, there was very little control over that "sail."

With the tide running one way, and the wind the other, the kid elected to go with the wind and against that current, and eased into that landing. He called over to the waiting men, lined up on that ladder, "Fellas, I'll only be able to hold close to that landing for a few moments at a time. When I say 'OK,' three or four of you jump aboard. When I see I'm losing it, I'll holler 'stop,' pull away, and make a new approach."

That landing craft, like a skittery pony, didn't know whether to respond to that current, or that wind, or those waves. But the boy captain was in command. Two, or three, or sometimes four men would jump aboard, the kid would see he was starting to lose it, would halt the loading, pull away, and then set up another approach.

When all the men were finally aboard, he headed for the inner harbor, a quiet, older man sitting near him. The run settled into its steady hum. The quiet man spoke, "That was some show you put on back there; I've never seen such skill with a small boat. You've done this before?"

"Yes," the kid replied, surprised, and yet pleased that anyone noticed. "I used to run tugs on the Columbia River."

"I *see*," said the quiet man.

The Army

"But you, Sir," the kid queried, "You know boating; what is your position on the ship?"

"Oh, I'm the captain," came the gentle reply, a very faint smile on his lips.

And for that seven-mile run to the inner harbor, a kid tugboat skipper and an old sea captain were one, there on the backwaters of the Yellow Sea.

Funny Things

There were funny things that happened on the Army boats too. The narrowly averted tragedy was the collision between one of the Army LCVPs and a loaded Korean 60- or 70-foot junk.

There was so little wind, generally, back there on that Yellow Sea, that the junks had incredibly tall masts, maybe two or three masts over a hundred feet tall, on a 50- or 60-foot boat. Always they could be seen, plying up and down the waterways and sea, often with all or most of the family also sculling the craft along. On each little ship there would be three or four sculling stations. Instead of rowing, as we would a rowboat, a long oar, or sweep, trailed astern; on the upper end, a handle angled off to the lower side. As the oarsman pushed back and forth on that handle, the sweep would angle back and forth, something like a single blade of a propeller moving back and forth, but reversing its pitch each time, so that it always pushed aft, shoving the boat along. They were graceful things to watch, and most of the G.I. operators gave them a fairly wide berth.

But always there was the daredevil, or perhaps a better name, the smart aleck, who tried to see how close he could "buzz" those boats. The Koreans would just wave and grin. They were used to accommodating to occupying armies. But one night, one of the Army boys buzzed too close and tore the side out of a 60- or 70-foot junk loaded with bags of salt. The family aboard was saved, and I'm sure the U.S. Army paid very well for a sunken, Korean ship, but hundreds of bags of salt were scattered around by those surging tides.

The bags were of woven grass, so most broke, dumped their salt, and floated to the surface. And for several nights after that, charging water taxis would run over one of those floating bags, unseen in the dark, and pick it up in their propeller. For a few moments, that little ship would shake like a rat terrier shaking a rat, and all aboard were certain they had hit a mine. It was terribly disconcerting. A shut down, and reversing of the prop, would clear the web; but it left many of the boy skippers both laughing over, and cursing that careless operator who buzzed too close one night.

Beer

Stealing, even in the Army, was stealing. But scrounging was, somehow, not a real offense. On their nights off, the kid and his Army boy crew would go scrounging.

One night they spied an LSM (a 203-foot Landing Ship Medium) tied, stern-to, to the side of a ship. They were loading cases of beer, thousands of cases. For some reason, their ramp was down and level, about four feet off the water. Huge lights flooded the work area above, and a uniformed and armed MP (Military Police) was pacing back and forth, guarding the cargo. But down by the ramp was darkness. As the kid eased up to the ramp, a Navy LCVP stealing, I mean "scrounging" beer, backed away in alarm. Well, that was his problem. The kid's deckhand caught a line, and he and the engineer started a "bucket brigade" loading beer.

They had eight or 10 cases aboard when the Navy, observing from off there in the dark that the Army boys were fellow criminals, came rushing back in. But the Navy coxswain over-shot his landing; his steel ramp clanged, like a loud alarm, against the steel ramp of the LSM. That MP up in the floodlights snapped to alert, and then started running down those stair steps of beer cases. The kid yelled at his crew, they threw two more cases aboard and tried to untie the line. It was jammed.

"That's OK," quietly called the kid, "get aboard." He gave a little slack, and backed full, the line breaking with a snap. The Army had more lines. And the boys flew away into the night, and safety.

The Army

Twelve cases of beer. Who said piracy didn't pay?

Army Boats Are Tough Too

The LCVP had been leaking some; the boys couldn't find the leak. One day, with an Army Transportation Corp officer aboard, they had been lying alongside an LCT, a small, low, power barge, that was alongside the ship the officer had been inspecting. The three boys and the officer were down inside their own boat, deciding where the officer needed to go next. The scratching sound of a near propeller telegraphed up through the hull; but that was common enough. But then the shock of hearing a voice, almost overhead saying, "Well, she was a pretty boat, wasn't she?"

All four dashed topside to the shock of seeing a towering, 203-foot LSM sliding in on them. Intending to make a downstream landing alongside the ship, the skipper had miscalculated the current drift. The kid's deckhand untied the boat, but it was clear there was no time for escape, so all four abandoned ship, and stepped over onto the LCT.

As that big ship slid into that tiny boat, the sounds of splintering wood and screeching of metal, told them their boat was gone. But only a few moments later, the LSM was sprung back away by the resilient side of that little boat, and it started to drift away. The deckhand was closest, and seeing no water in the boat, jumped aboard, started the engine, and ran it back up alongside the LCT. Someone caught a line, and they inspected their damaged craft.

As with that Russell tug, a few years before, they could find not a sign of broken wood, not a mark anywhere, no water coming in. So they ran home to the dock in the inner harbor. Days later they noted that their boat no longer had that nagging leak. Wooden boats are resilient.

Home

One day, the announcement came: "All men with three children or more at home can apply for discharge tomorrow morning." The kid was one of the first in line. And a few weeks later, he was being discharged at again, Fort Lewis, in Washington State. His service to his country was now history. The tugs of the Columbia River were waiting. It was good to be home.

Chapter 28

General Construction

A Miserable Job

General Construction Company was, and is, a good outfit. The kid worked two different jobs for them; one, the most miserable tug job he'd ever held, and the other, the most fun tug job he'd ever held. Let's talk about that miserable one first to dispose of it, but also to show that there could be dark days on the river, which only showed in contrast the glory of the bright days.

The *Philip R.* was a dying tug, very literally coming apart at the seams. She was really beyond repair, so the carpenters patched her up as best they could, and the machinists installed a pair of heavy-duty, one and a half-inch pumps to keep her from sinking. One pump worked off the engine when underway; the other was an electric pump for the time she was tied to the dredge. The first two things when coming in for a landing were to catch a line and plug in that electric pump.

General had the contract for pumping sand from the floor of the Columbia River, and laying it along the shore for the bed for the new, water-grade highway that Oregon State was building from Portland to The Dalles. They were working in the Hood River area with a 24-inch pipeline suction dredge, when the kid went aboard as the second skipper, working one of the two 12-hour shifts.

There were a number of things that added up to make that a miserable job. The kid had had some health problems that left him with just a bit less emotional energy than the special challenges of that particular set of job circumstances demanded. And, although the superintendent, Otto Roeder, was a brilliant engineer, he was also a gentle, kind man, preferring to let power struggles among the crew, "work themselves out." And added to all that, the skipper already on the job, though a good operator, had backed off, and let those dredge deckhands fill the authority vacuum with their own, cocky arrogance; the kind that develop when little men get the upper hand.

The kid had clearly been set up by fate. He had walked into a tugboat quagmire, and, like the *Philip R.*, was beset with storms beyond the given capabilities of his damaged, personal ship.

He weathered that storm and held on for several months, until a job as manager of the Port of Klickitat County was handed to him. The kid now had time, and the safety of harbor, to effect repairs, and he did.

But running that *Philip R.* was a miserable job.

On the Beach

On the beach, yes, but managing the Port was a good job. The kid was at home every night, working civilized hours, eating well, and getting his rest. And his mind was challenged to turn a drifting Port Authority into an organized entity. He had a tough, old logger, named Joe Crow, on the Port Commission. Joe was on the kid's side, and together they got the political and organizational machinery going; and a truly operating Port was begun at Bingen, Washington, in western Klickitat County.

But the Heavenly plans for the kid's life did not call for him to remain in the safety of a harbor indefinitely.

True, a man, like a ship, in the harbor is safe, but that is not what either was created for. It is written, "All things work together for good to them who love God." When politics raised its manipulative head, and the kid was muscled out in favor of a retired Forest

Service supervisor, it seemed like a dirty deal. But the kid had regained his health, and he and that grand, tough, old logger, Joe Crow, had gotten the ship, called the Klickitat County Port District Number One, underway.

It was time to go back to the waters.

The *Paula Jean*

> "Paula Jean was long and lean, with features fair and glancing. I took her out, one stormy night, for moonlight cruise—and dancing..."

So goes the ballad the kid wrote years later about that marvelous little tug. She was probably the most fun tug the kid ever ran. But, exactly opposite from the *Philip R.* story, this time there were a number of things that added up to make that a fun job.

The kid had his health, radiant and ready for the challenge; and, the Paula Jean, though small, was alive. Forty feet of tough steel, with a 12-foot beam, she had, I believe, a 225 hp Superior diesel. Only 225 hp, but they were big horses. An excellent propeller that gave her as much power in reverse as ahead, and monkey rudders, for excellent steering when backing, even with a load, together, gave her a versatility limited only by the imagination and skill of her captain. And one more thing: "Irish" Alphin was job superintendent. Anyone who remembers "Irish," even if they had had some bad experiences with him, had to agree, on any job on which "Irish" was superintendent, there was only one chief in the tribe. The kid, and the opposite shift skipper, we'll call him Jeff, were captains of their ship. Only one man gave them orders. Everyone else asked. That is the way a captain is supposed to command.

But we're getting ahead of the story. This time, General Construction had the contract to build the coffer dam to protect the building of the power houses during construction of the Dalles Dam. On leaving the port, the kid almost immediately stepped into the wheelhouse of the *Paula Jean* as captain. It was perfect timing.

Geography or Geology

Geologists tell us that in quite recent geologic time, the area around The Dalles was flooded with a flow of molten basalt rock. As the river cut a new channel through that stone, curious things happened. For example, right where the dam was being built, the river had cut a deep (280 feet, in places) channel, sometimes nearly as deep as it was wide. But right in that vicinity the channel made three, sharp, 90-degree turns, the middle, and most severe, immediately above the power house to be; that is, the channel running southeast, turned abruptly 90 degrees to the southwest for a mile or so. The power house was to dump southward into the Washington side of that southwest-flowing channel. Of course the coffer dam was being built there.

On the inside of that sharp "L," was a small, solid stone island a couple hundred feet across, the main course of the current going outside, or on the "L," side of the island. Only a very small flow ran between the island and the stone of the Washington shore. And this all added up to an ideal location for making the up to 40 or 50 barge moves a day that the *Paula Jean* routinely made; quiet, deep water, with very little current below the protection of that island. There was only one "thorn" in this barge juggler's heaven. That west wind came right off that coffer dam, unrestricted. And when it piped up to 25 to 40 knots, as it could do, there were some real challenges. But more of that later.

A Challenging Game

With five rigs to tend (that is, two huge derrick barges and three drill rigs drilling the rock and planting dynamite) and also a fuel barge and two or three barges for steel sheet piling and other supplies, that little tug was kept, happily, very busy. Each rig had its distinctive whistle, and when they called, the kid just wrote them down on a note pad and took them in turn. "I'm only one tug, guys, you'll have to wait your turns." Generally the pilebuck foreman understood. But the kid and his skilled counterpart, Jeff, developed

General Construction

the smooth routines where they were making sometimes four complete barge moves an hour. That included making up to a tow, moving it up or down, generally without turning around, because of that excellent control astern, tying up the tow, cutting loose, and going to the next. It was a real game.

Two Flaws Collide

"But if, when you do well, and suffer for it, you take it patiently, this is acceptable with God." 1 Peter 2:20.

Irish was generally fair—strong, direct, even blunt at times—but fair. "*How* you run that tug, kid, is your business." But like any man, sometimes when the pressures built, he could get crotchety, to put it mildly. And Jeff, though a superb operator, and generally reliable, would occasionally nip the jug too much. To put it kindly, it interfered with his reliability. One midnight crew change time, those two flaws collided, and the kid innocently was caught in the middle.

He had arrived at the site about 11:30 P.M. to relieve Jeff. But no tug was around. A foreman disgustedly pointed up and across the river. "The b_____s are over there asleep, or drunk, or both. We've been whistling for them for half an hour."

The last lock for the Celilo Canal emptied in to the river right at that "L." There was an eddy of quiet water there, and a landing for picking up the crews. The tug was at the landing. So the kid grabbed a skiff (rowboat) and rowed over. It took 20 or 30 minutes. In the meantime, someone had phoned Irish, in bed at home. The kid stepped into the wheelhouse and found two drunken Indians, sound asleep, the tug rumbling in gear against the dock. Jeff was about half Indian, and his drinking buddy that night was, ironically, another half Indian, a fine pilebuck foreman, and Irish's closest friend.

Before the kid could awaken the two truants, get them off the tug, and run for the rigs, a furious Irish Alphin stormed aboard. Friend or not, drinking buddy or not, innocent relieving skipper or not, all were helpless targets of that Irishman's wrath and scathing

113

tongue. The slightest attempt at defense by the kid was met with a renewed storm of fury. That formidable giant dragged those meek and silent children off the tug and then flung back at the kid, "If you expect to be working for General tomorrow, you'd better get your ___ back over to those rigs, and now."

The kid said, "Yes, sir," and backed away.

That Jug Again

I just can't say enough about that half Indian, Jeff. He was a superb operator. The kid was good, really good with that tug, but if possible, Jeff was better. But that cursed jug.

The Union pay scale for tugboatmen at the time was $1.56 an hour. For the pilebucks, $2.80. "I don't want those pilebucks touching that tug, kid," Irish would say, "They'll just break something."

"Then how about paying us pilebucks' pay?" the boys argued.

"Oh h___ boys, I can't do that. The union would grab that and run. We'd have to be paying all our skippers that. No, tell you what I will do; I'll *let* you work 12 hours a day. That will be eight hours straight time and four hours overtime."

The boys gave up and accepted the compromise.

It was a busy 12 hours, from 8:00 A.M. to about 8:00 P.M., but then things quieted down, and the skipper on duty could get catnaps, even an hour or so sleep at a time in the wee hours. The kid could be sound asleep for half an hour or so, hear a whistle, and be on his feet and running for the rig in seconds, wide awake. So he proposed to Jeff, "To save half the running to and from work (the kid was flying his airplane 25 miles up the river from White Salmon), let's each work 24 hours on and 24 hours off."

Jeff agreed. And for several months it worked wonderfully well—except when Jeff got drunk.

It probably didn't happen more than a dozen times or so; and anyway, the kid just couldn't get mad at that loveable, superb skipper-friend. But once in a while the kid would run to the landing for the 8:00 A.M. crew, after his 24-hour stint in the wheelhouse of that tug. No Jeff. So the kid would run Jeff's 24 hours. The next morning the kid would run to the landing for the crew, but, since it was the beginning of what would have been the kid's shift anyway, of course there was no Jeff. So the kid ran another 24 hours, surviving on that three or four hours total napping time during the night.

On the third morning, Jeff would be there, haggard, pale faced, his head obviously throbbing. When he let the kid off to go to his airplane and home, Jeff would plaintively ask, "When you comin' back, Cap?"

And the kid would cheerily answer, "Oh, I don't know, Jeff, in two or three days, I guess."

And Jeff would just moan, and back away. And then the captain in him would take control. He really was a good man.

The Captain and the Leverman

The leverman on the derrick barge, *Astoria*, was special. He was young, although several years older than the kid, and he was sharp. Not only was he a good leverman, trusted completely by the men who had to work under and around the steel piling and other heavy loads the rig lifted, he had been around long enough to learn the quite different characteristics of that free-floating barge when under the control of the tug.

The *Paula Jean*'s wheelhouse was right on the deck; the skipper's eyes not over eight feet above the water. Made up to the stern of the *Astoria*, with its huge house blocking all view for 160 degrees ahead, the skipper had to rely on signals from pilebuck deckhands, often given too late; or, if he was fortunate, he had this sharp leverman up in the control cab of the rig.

After a number of moves, he and the kid learned each other. A trust and a oneness developed between these two men that was marvelous. Whether that leverman was operating the tug by hand signals from his full-view platform, or whether the kid was "seeing" the unseen through the hand signals of that leverman, neither really knew, or cared. But they found that they could put that huge rig into some awfully tight places and not bump a thing.

The Thorn in the Barge Juggler's Heaven

The other derrick barge, the *Frisco*, was really a 500-ton "shipyard" crane, set on a steel barge. Although she would swing in the wind, as a later story tells, it was the *Astoria* that was a towering sail. Weighing much less than the *Frisco*, the *Astoria* had a house over her machinery that made for twice or three times the windage.

The *Astoria*'s crew had whistled for the tug. "Just a simple move, Cap," the pilebuck foreman said. "We want 'er in against the beach over there a couple hundred feet." She was secured against the most recently built "cell" in the continuing coffer dam.

Those "cells" were built of sheet piling, about a half-inch thick and about 16 inches wide, with an interlocking grip on each edge. A new piling was lifted high by one end, the pilebuck would guide that interlocking grip into the grip on the last piling in place, and then the new one was lowered to the river floor, the two grips holding hands to each other. The process continued in a circle about 30 feet across, making, in very real fact, a steel barrel, which was then filled with earth and gravel, thus building a strong, very effective coffer dam that could also be easily removed. The row of cells was about half completed.

But the "thorn" that was the west wind, was wild. The kid routinely made up to the stern of the *Astoria*, the pilebucks cut her loose; the kid poured on the power, trying to make that left turn into the beach only a few hundred feet away. The pilebuck foreman, a calm, intelligent, most cooperative, but very much in command foreman, would usually stay in the wheelhouse with the kid during these moves, so they could work together.

The *Astoria* was coming around into that wild wind, but she was also sliding badly to the right. The Number Four drill rig was only a few hundred feet further over, their crew getting worried.

"You know, John, I don't think we're going to make it," the kid calmly announced.

And John as calmly answered, "No, I don't think so either."

"Well, let's get out of here," the kid said, and threw the tug in reverse, and poured on the power. The *Astoria* slowly stopped, and

General Construction

then swung in a swoosh past that drill rig, and weathervaned out to the river. With that powerful reverse, the kid could easily back toward the beach. But they wanted the rig turned around. The two men looked at each other and thought.

"You know, John, the kid said, "We can back up to that cell again. Your boys can take an anchor line from that port corner and hang the rig off on that. I can run around to the forward end and take a line from there over to the beach, and you can then pull yourselves in."

That shrewd pilebuck foreman barked orders, the kid did his work, and in 15 minutes the tug went on to its next move. That west wind could be a real thorn.

That Thorn Again

That northwest wind often piped up to that 25 to 30 knots in the afternoons, but it was only on rare occasions that it coincided with a heavy move. Sometime later, the *Frisco* had to be moved up river a half mile and put in against the Washington shore, just below the island. There was not time to call in one of the big tugs. That west wind was screaming. "Can you do it?" Irish asked.

The kid thought for a minute, listening to that inner spirit. "Yeah, we can do it," he answered.

He made up to the stern of the *Frisco*, his tiny tug looking more like just a motorboat tagged on behind that massive rig. The lines were cut loose, the *Frisco* swung away; that Superior diesel barked at full power.

The kid had learned some lessons with the *Astoria*. The *Frisco* was much heavier, yet with some less windage, and he had a half mile in which to take control and plan his final move, that crucial landing into a narrow slot on the Washington shore just before that island.

They charged up that flat river, the tow crabbing into the wind. He could hold it there OK, but that wind was coming at an angle from the left. The final stop and landing would be a balancing act. There would be no way on the tow, and so almost no steering control. It was only two or three hundred feet from the island to that unforgiving, rocky landing on the north shore.

The kid knew he would have to go as close as possible to the island before turning in order to get that crucial angle into the wind. He counted on that small current coming down between the island and the north shore to help in the final turn. How far did the underwater reef, indicated by the surface rock, extend down from the island? The kid estimated 200 feet.

The young captain watched and waited and listened for that spirit. The island grew closer, only seconds to go now, surely. Now, now, hard left, hard. The *Frisco* came around, slowly, sliding toward that island. Finally her nose reached into that current, the deep barge responded, swinging to the left. But just as the starboard, stern corner of the barge was clearing the reef, the kid felt a definite thump. That steel barge was tough, the kid let it pass; there was a crucial landing yet to make. But his Guardian Angel gently reminded him that he had crowded his margins mighty close.

They charged into that small cove at full power, not quite balanced into the wind as he needed to be. There was one last card in his hand. As he shut down and kicked the gear into reverse, he also turned hard right rudder. That superb propeller slowed the rushing barge, and slamming the wheelwash against those monkey rudders, pulled the stern to the right. As the bow of that barge touched the beach, the whole tow was directly into the wind. It was an exciting demonstration of tugboating skill; and congratulations came. But the kid knew, when he felt that barge bump just the corner of that reef, that he had borrowed again into that special loan program. He had some saving up to do.

He was not given much time.

A Better Story to Tell

It wasn't that west wind this time that presented the challenge. It was a rising river, and that sharp, 90-degree turn in a rushing, narrow stream.

General Construction

The coffer dam job was coming to an end. A big tug had taken the *Frisco* up around the corner for some final work. That work was finished; the river was flooding, the *Frisco* had to come out.

"Kid," Irish challenged, "You can bring 'er out."

"Good grief, Irish, I can barely get up there empty; what are you saying?" All prudence cried in the kid's ear, "No, no, no."

"Well, come and look it over with me," Irish pleaded. "We've got to get 'er out today, and I can't get a big tug till tomorrow." So they drove over in the company pickup.

"Now I figure," Irish began, "We can get you made up, turn the rig loose, and you should have time to get turned around before you have to make the turn at the corner . . ." Irish didn't get a chance to finish his statement. The kid had been studying, and thinking.

"Irish," the kid interrupted, with an authority beyond his years, "*if* I'm going to do it, I won't turn her around first; I'll let the current push us down and let the tug push into the eddy by the locks. As the current spins the barge past the island, I'll pour it on and hope we can get some way on her before we crash against that cliff on the Oregon shore."

"OK, OK, Cap," Irish protested, knowing he had challenged this boy tugboatman, who had proven his skills to an old veteran construction man. "I'm not telling you how to run your tug. Get hooked on. I'll get the crew ready."

The kid was driven back for his tug; his mental computer already starting to work out the plan, his mind actually seeing the plan executed. But as he ran up to that rig with the tug, he was poignantly aware that he needed one-half to three-quarters throttle just to hold the light tug against that current. Some pilebucks helped him make up to the rig.

Like a bronc rider readying for the opening of that chute, his engine full ahead, the kid poised and waited. The last line was free; the tow rushed downstream backwards, toward that menacing turn.

Although the current must have been coming down around 10 mph, the tug was pushing up around five, so he had some control. He eased over to the right, deliberately setting up the river to force the tug into that eddy. It worked; the kid kicked his engine out of gear. Like a towering, massive pendulum, that huge derrick barge swung broadside to that current, slamming down toward the stony cliff that turned the entire Columbia River abruptly, 90 degrees to the west. That water was boiling.

But again, that inner spirit had to do the computing. He had to clear that island, on the southeast side this time, before he could push safely past. But he also knew that, because of the simple inertia of getting several hundred tons of steel and machinery moving, he would have to begin his final move before they cleared the island. Too soon, he might clip the island; too late, and he could not get way on, and thus control to hold off that high cliff. He waited. He could not see directly ahead.

The plan had been discussed with a pilebuck shift foreman with whom the kid worked well.

"Jimmy, you stay up forward, and as soon as you are sure we can pour it on and not hit the island, give me the sign."

The seconds seemed long; the kid waited. But they were only seconds.

Jimmy's arms waved, "Go for it, go," he yelled.

"OK, baby," the kid spoke lovingly to his little ship, "It's up to you now, let's go." He gave her full power, but only 30 degrees or so of right rudder. He had to stop that swing, yes, but more, he had to get moving. The Columbia River, all of it, boiled against that unmoving shore, barely 200 feet away. The tow began to move. The space dropped to 150 feet, then 100, then 75. But they were moving. The narrowing margin held, and then slowly widened. They had made it. A cheer went up from the crew on the rig.

When they landed the *Frisco* in the quiet water below, Irish didn't say thank you to the kid. But he had just a hint of a grin around his lips, as he gave his next order. There was a bit of daring kid in that tough, old superintendent for General Construction Company.

Later, that favorite pilebuck foreman said to the kid, "You know, I wouldn't wish trouble on anyone, but wouldn't we have had a story to tell our grandkids if we had dumped the *Frisco* into 280 feet of water at The Dalles Dam?"

The kid laughed at the suggestion, but he was glad it turned out this way. It's a better story to tell.

Chapter 29
The Final Story

After The Dalles Dam, the kid left the river for a while to be closer to his family, and worked as an assistant electrical engineer for an electric utility, there in White Salmon.

But then, the airplane and its magic wings, the lure of the last frontier, called him to the North. He began a new career as an air traffic control specialist for the Federal Aviation Agency, in Anchorage, Alaska.

But he never really left the waters, but kept his seamanship alive with motorboats and the exacting art of sailing, and, of course, with an occasional boat job with "Foss," or the Alaska Department of Fish and Game.

He even won, in an eight-race series regatta, the coveted Alaska Governor's Cup Sailing Trophy; and he did it on his 65th birthday. A remarkable achievement, and a dramatic story in itself. But then, it is not the story of a kid on the river. It shall be told another day.

———

The screaming engines had quieted some, as the big plane made its last turn before settling on final approach to Portland International Airport. We were crossing the Columbia, and as always, I scanned the water for some memory, some small link with the past. There, that small tug, with a single log raft, plodding down that great waterway. I smiled and thought of a kid I once knew,

The Final Story

long ago, and the rich and varied experiences he had had as a boy tugboat captain on that historic stream.

And now the final story can be told. I was, of course, that kid. And the "kid's" dad was Captain Luke Nichols, to whom this book is lovingly, even reverently dedicated.

And the "kid's" first real tug was the exceptionally well designed, and remarkable handling tug, the *Louise N.*, a 38-foot, wooden vessel, with a 60 hp Atlas diesel. She was named after my sister, Louise Nichols, Mrs. Jack Frederick.

Again, it is my prayer that no one named in this book, or relative of anyone named in this book, will take any offense. Most surely, none at all has been intended.

And I ask one more thing, surely the most important of all.

There has been a thread woven through this story, an unbroken thread. If you missed it, you have missed something of inestimable value. If you found it, you have found that elastic, yet indestructible strand that is life itself. Cling to that thread; cling to life.

Capt. Dean Nichols
The kid on the river

Kid on the River